MUSIC AND SONGWRITING FOR TEENS: A STEP-BY-STEP SYSTEM

FROM BLANK PAGE TO FIRST SONG, WRITE LYRICS, CHORDS, AND HOOKS LIKE YOUR FAVORITE ARTISTS (NO EXPERIENCE NEEDED!)

WILLIAM J. CALLAGHAN

CONTENTS

"Nobody should feel pressured to be 'good' at art. Just make stuff that makes you feel something."

— BILLIE EILISH

"Write like no one's listening, because at first, no one is. That's where the magic happens."

— OLIVIA RODRIGO

INTRODUCTION

You're sitting there, staring at a blank page. Your pen hovers above the paper, or your fingers tap on your phone screen. You've got a melody stuck in your head and emotions swirling in your chest, but no words come out. You wonder if you'll ever turn this jumble of thoughts and tunes into a real song. Sound familiar?

Welcome to *Music and Songwriting for Teens*. This book is your guide to transforming those musical ideas into actual songs. And here's the best part—you don't need to be a prodigy or have fancy equipment. This book is made for ordinary teens, whether you're scribbling lyrics during lunch or recording tunes on your phone. We want to make songwriting accessible and empowering for anyone with a story.

Many teens face the same hurdles when it comes to songwriting. Self-doubt creeps in. You might think, *"Am I good enough?"* or *"What if people don't like it?"* Then there's the technical stuff—chords, progressions, and hooks—that can feel like learning a new language. It's easy to feel overwhelmed and give up. But guess what?

You're not alone.

This book has a step-by-step system that breaks everything down into bite-sized, manageable steps. We'll go through lyrics, chords, and hooks in a way that makes sense. You'll learn to turn your emotions into lyrics that resonate, understand chords without needing a piano, and create hooks that stick in listeners' heads— and on platforms like TikTok.

What makes this book different? It's not filled with complex jargon or endless music theory lessons. Instead, it's action-oriented. Its goal is to build your confidence and spark your creativity. We focus on what you can do now with what you have. There is no fluff, just real steps you can take to make your music.

We know that every teenager has a unique voice and story. You might write poetry during math class or hum melodies while waiting for the bus. This book meets you where you are. Songwriting is for everyone who wants to capture their voice and harness their creativity. Your music matters, and your ideas are worth sharing!

You may dream of expressing yourself through music and connecting with others who feel the same. Perhaps you want to share your story and have it resonate. This book is here to remind you that your voice is valid. Your creativity is essential. You can do this!

Think of this as a journey, not just a how-to guide. You'll learn to own your songwriting process and build skills that boost your confidence. We'll help you develop your creative identity and discover what makes your music unique.

When you turn the last page, you won't just understand songwriting. You'll also feel empowered to create music that reflects who you truly are. Whether it's your first song or your fiftieth, this book is here to support you every step of the way. Let's get started. Your music is closer than you think.

1

LAYING THE FOUNDATION

Have you ever sat with your guitar, fingers poised, or maybe just your phone in hand, trying to capture that perfect melody swirling in your head? The room is quiet, save for your humming and the soft scratching of pen on paper. But as the minutes tick by, doubt creeps in. Why can't you find the right words? Can you even call yourself a songwriter if you can't finish a verse? These moments of uncertainty are part of the creative process, not a sign that you're not cut out for this.

Songwriting doesn't need loads of talent or fancy equipment. You need to find your voice and learn how to express it. This chapter is your starting point, helping you lay a solid foundation for your songwriting journey. We will explore how to embrace your inner songwriter by acknowledging and overcoming self-doubt, understanding your musical influences, and developing a unique creative identity. These building blocks will support you as you grow into a confident songwriter.

EMBRACING YOUR INNER SONGWRITER

Self-doubt is like an unwelcome guest who shows up uninvited. It whispers that you're not good enough, that someone else could do it better—that maybe you should give up. But here's the truth: every songwriter, from beginners to megastars, grapples with self-doubt. The key is not to let it stop you. You must transform that nagging internal dialogue into something positive and true. Start by catching those negative thoughts and flipping them into positive affirmations. Instead of *"I can't do this,"* try *"I'm learning and growing."* Celebrate small wins; each written line and melody hummed is progress. Practice mindfulness or meditation to center yourself and clear your clutter, allowing mental space for creativity to flourish.

Music has shaped who you are in ways you might not even recognize yet. Think about those songs that make your heart race or bring tears to your eyes. They leave an imprint, influencing how you perceive the world and express yourself. Creating a musical influence map can help you see these connections more clearly. List your favorite artists and songs, noting the emotions they stir in you. Understanding these emotional responses lets you see how they might weave into your music. This exercise doesn't involve copying your idols but recognizing how their music resonates with you and using it as a springboard for creativity.

Defining your artistic style is like finding your musical fingerprint. It's discovering what makes your music uniquely yours. Start with journaling exercises to reflect on your interests, experiences, and what you want your music to say. Explore diverse musical elements, different genres, or instruments that intrigue you. This exploration will help you build a creative identity that feels authentic. Remember, it's okay if this process takes time because creativity isn't a race.

A growth mindset can make all the difference in approaching challenges and setbacks in your songwriting. Having a growth mindset means viewing abilities as something you can develop rather than something fixed. Embrace challenges as opportunities to gain experience rather than obstacles to fear (Revart, 2023). When you hit a roadblock, see it as a chance to innovate and experiment with new techniques. Each failure isn't a setback but a stepping stone toward improvement. Even the most accomplished artists have pieces they're less proud of—what matters is their willingness to learn from those moments.

Reflection Exercise: Your Creative Compass

Take a moment to reflect on these questions: *What emotions do I want my music to evoke? How do my favorite songs influence my sound? What unique perspective do I bring to my songwriting?* Jot down your thoughts in a journal or note-taking app. Use this as your creative compass, guiding each step of your songwriting process.

By embracing who you are as an artist, recognizing the influences that have shaped you, and cultivating a mindset that welcomes growth and learning, you build a solid foundation to support your creative endeavors. Whether it's battling self-doubt or exploring new musical landscapes, each step will bring you closer to crafting songs that are unapologetically yours.

THE EMOTIONAL PALETTE

Think of emotions as colors on your creative palette, each hue adding richness and depth to your songwriting canvas. To paint with feeling, you must first recognize which emotions drive your creative process. Start by identifying core emotions that resonate with you. Are you drawn to the melancholy of a rainy day, or do you thrive on the joy of a sunlit afternoon? Emotion mapping exercises can help. Take a piece of paper and sketch your feelings as they come to you. Label them and explore their origins—was it something someone said or a memory that resurfaced without warning? Visualizing emotions lets you see patterns and connections that inform your lyrical storytelling.

Translating these emotions into lyrics is where the real magic happens. You want to capture the essence of your feelings and express them in words that resonate. One effective way is through metaphor and simile. These literary tools allow you to draw parallels between your feelings and tangible images. For instance, you might imagine heartache as a storm brewing in the distance or happiness as a kite dancing in the wind. Workshops focusing on these techniques can sharpen your skills, helping you create vivid, relatable lyrics. Writing prompts are also helpful; consider scenarios where emotions run high, like standing on the edge of a fantastic opportunity or reflecting on a bittersweet goodbye. Let sensory details seep into your lyrics—describe the wind's chill or the warmth of sunlight to evoke emotions in your listeners.

Balancing raw emotion with structured songwriting elements is necessary for coherence. While emotions fuel creativity, the structure gives it form. Think of emotional anchor points within your song structure—moments where emotion peaks, like the chorus or bridge. These anchors tie your song together, making it more impactful. Dynamic contrast can also enhance emotional depth. Play with volume, tempo, and intensity to mirror emotional shifts within your song. A quiet verse followed by an explosive chorus can take listeners on an emotional rollercoaster that heightens engagement and resonance.

Emotions can overwhelm, but they can also be harnessed positively. Use them as fuel rather than letting them take control.

Transform negative emotions into creative energy by channeling them into your work. If angry or frustrated, let those feelings guide your writing and transform chaos into art. Practicing emotional detachment can provide clarity; try to step back from intense emotions to see them objectively. This distance will allow you to understand and translate emotions into lyrics more effectively without being swept away.

Let's look at a scenario that could happen in real life: Imagine sitting in your school cafeteria, surrounded by noise and chatter, but feeling utterly alone. That loneliness isn't just a mood; it's also an emotion ready to be explored. Grab a napkin or open the notes app on your phone. Start jotting down how this loneliness feels—like an echo in an empty room or a shadow at dusk. Don't worry if it doesn't make sense; you capture the raw emotions. Later, these fragments can become verses or hooks that carry your song's emotional weight.

You might find that specific emotions recur in your work—perhaps nostalgia weaves through every melody, or hope springs eternal in your choruses. That's okay; it means you're finding your emotional voice. These emotions will become more precise and refined each time you write, shaping your unique sound and style.

Remember, every emotion you feel has the potential to add depth to your music. Embrace, map, and translate them into lyrics that can speak to others. Balance them with structure so that they resonate without overwhelming the listeners. With practice, you'll find that emotions are not just something to be felt but tools to be wielded creatively. They're what makes your songs not merely *heard* but also *felt* deeply by anyone who listens.

SETTING THE STAGE WITH SONGWRITING TOOLS

In songwriting, having the right tools can make a big difference. For example, using a notebook and pen can help you organize your ideas and capture inspiration whenever it strikes. A notebook is where you can brainstorm lyrics, sketch out melodies, or write down any creative thoughts that come to mind. Writing by hand can also help you slow down and think more clearly, making your ideas stronger and more personal. Whether working in your room or on the go, having a dedicated place to keep your songwriting notes is smart.

However, let's not forget the power of technology. Digital Audio Workstations, or DAWs, are game-changers for modern songwriters. These software platforms—like GarageBand or Audacity—allow you to record, edit, and mix music from your laptop or tablet. They're user-friendly, and many offer free versions, making them accessible to those just starting. Imagine layering sounds, tweaking effects, and hearing your song come to life with just a few clicks. DAWs open doors to experimentation, letting you try new things without fear of mistakes.

For those interested in recording, affordable equipment like USB microphones or basic audio interfaces can significantly enhance the quality of your projects. These tools don't have to break the bank; many budget-friendly options deliver impressive sound quality. A good pair of headphones can also make a significant difference, allowing you to hear every detail. With these essentials, you'll be well-equipped to capture your songs in a way that does them justice.

Technology enhances creativity in ways previously unimaginable. Music production software offers endless possibilities for arranging and customizing tracks. You can experiment with different instruments and sounds you might not have physical access to. Online collaborative platforms like Soundtrap or BandLab are great for connecting with other musicians, sharing ideas, and even co-writing songs remotely. This connectivity means you're never creating alone; there's an entire world of inspiration and feedback at your fingertips.

Keeping an organized toolkit is vital for efficiency and focus. Start by establishing a resolute digital or physical workspace where your tools are easily accessible. A tidy desk with artfully arranged equipment can make all the difference when you're in the creative zone. Categorize resources in folders on your computer or use physical binders for printed materials. Having everything in order will mean less time spent searching and more time creating.

As your skills grow, so should your collection of tools. Gradually investing in advanced equipment can elevate your craft. Perhaps save up for a higher-quality guitar or keyboard that offers more versatility than beginner models. Explore advanced software options that provide deeper editing capabilities or unique sound libraries. Expand thoughtfully, ensuring each addition enhances your music-making process.

Let's say you've been using the same guitar since you first started playing—it's familiar and comfortable. But as you get deeper into songwriting, you might crave new sounds or a better range. Saving for an upgrade (or making a birthday wish list to give your relatives!) advances your skills and renews your passion for playing. Similarly, trying out different DAWs might unlock features that align perfectly with your evolving style.

Let's consider the case of Ella, a high school student who started writing songs using her smartphone's voice memo app and a school-issued laptop. She began with simple tools: a second-hand notebook and GarageBand on her device. Over time, as her confidence grew, she invested in a MIDI keyboard and a quality microphone. Each new tool brought fresh inspiration and opportunities for creativity that Ella hadn't imagined.

Try to create an environment where creativity can thrive by setting yourself up with the right tools and learning how to use technology to your advantage. Great songs often start with simple ideas—a line in a notebook, a voice memo, or a few chords on a phone app. Your toolkit doesn't need to be fancy; what matters is how you use it to express your unique voice.

Take Billie Eilish, for example. She and her brother Finneas started recording music in their bedroom using basic gear and free software like GarageBand. They kept things simple, but they knew how to use their tools well, and that's how hits like "Ocean Eyes" were born. As you organize and expand your setup, you'll be ready to shape your raw ideas into complete songs and bring your musical visions to life.

CREATING A SONGWRITING SANCTUARY

The environment you create can significantly impact your creativity. It's like the difference between trying to solve math problems in a noisy cafeteria versus a quiet library. To unleash your songwriting prowess, you need a space that fuels your imagination and keeps you comfortable. Start by selecting a dedicated area for songwriting. It may be a corner of your room or a sunny nook by the window. This space doesn't have to be large or fancy, just somewhere you can associate it with creativity. Personalize it with things that inspire you—posters of your favorite bands, photos that evoke emotions, or quotes that resonate with your artistic vision.

Comfort and functionality are also important. The basics are a chair that can support you comfortably through long sessions, a desk for your equipment, and maybe a soft lamp for ambient lighting. Ensure everything you need is within arm's reach. The goal is to create a zone where distractions are minimized, allowing you to focus on the music.

Distractions are creativity's arch-nemesis. They can pull you out of the zone faster than a phone notification during your favorite movie scene. Implement time management techniques like setting specific hours for songwriting when you're least likely to be interrupted. You might find that early mornings or late nights work best when the world is quiet, and your mind is free to wander.

Establishing boundaries with family and friends can also help. Let them know when you're diving into your music and ask them to respect this time. Explain that you're not shutting them out but carving out moments for uninterrupted creation. Consider using noise-cancelling headphones or putting your phone on airplane mode to maintain focus.

Incorporating rituals and routines can signal the start of a creative session, like stretching before a run prepares your body for exercise, or taking a warm shower prepares you for sleep. Develop pre-songwriting habits that match your style, including listening to music that inspires you, reviewing old lyrics, or setting up your space to minimize distractions. Scheduling regular time blocks for songwriting can also help train your brain to enter a creative mindset more easily and consistently.

Singer-songwriter Taylor Swift has spoken about her habit of writing lyrics and melodies as soon as inspiration strikes, often late at night or early in the morning when things are quiet. She keeps notebooks nearby and regularly uses the Voice Memos app on her phone to capture ideas in the moment. Her process shows how simple, consistent routines can support creativity and make turning thoughts into fully developed songs easier.

Generating a positive atmosphere involves more than just tweaking your physical surroundings; you also want to cultivate an emotional space that motivates you. Natural light can do wonders for your mood, so position your workspace near a window where sunlight streams in. If natural light isn't an option, get some warm lighting options that mimic daylight, such as lamps. Adding plants can also enhance your environment by bringing life, freshness, and color into your space.

Sound is another way to create ambiance. Use music and sound-scapes to set the tone for your sessions. Maybe you prefer the gentle rustle of leaves or the soft patter of rain as background noise while you write. These soundscapes can help drown out distractions and immerse you in the creative process.

Creating a songwriting space means setting up an environment that supports focus, comfort, and creativity. This can be as simple as a quiet corner of your room with a desk, a comfortable chair, and the necessary tools, like a notebook, instrument, or recording device. Personal touches like good lighting, inspiring quotes, or even posters of your favorite artists can make the space feel more inviting and help you get into the right mindset.

For example, after school, having a dedicated space where you regularly go to write music can create a mental cue that it's time to focus. Over time, your brain will associate that space with creativity and productivity, making it easier to enter a flow state. The more you use it, the stronger that connection will become. It doesn't have to be a fancy studio; what matters is that it's yours, is consistent, and encourages you to work on your music.

As you cultivate this environment, remember that creativity is an evolving process. Your needs will change, and so should your space. Stay attuned to what fuels your inspiration, and don't be afraid to adjust as necessary. After all, songwriting is about finding comfort in expression, and there's no better place to start than in a sanctuary crafted just for you, by you.

2

MUSIC THEORY MADE SIMPLE

DEMYSTIFYING CHORDS AND PROGRESSIONS

When playing an instrument like the guitar or piano and working on a melody, your chords and progressions help shape the overall sound. A melody can feel flat or incomplete without the proper harmonic support. Chords provide a song's foundation and mood, helping reinforce the emotional tone and guide how the listener experiences the music. Understanding how chords are built and move from one to another, known as chord progressions, is essential to songwriting. Let's start with the basics of chord structure to see how it all works.

Chords are essentially groups of notes played together, and understanding them will unlock a new dimension in your music. The triad is the most common chord type, consisting of three notes played simultaneously. Think of them as building blocks. You start with a root note, add a third note above it, and then stack a fifth note on top. This simple combination can create significant, minor, or even more complex chords. Major chords are the go-to when you want your music to feel bright and uplifting. They're like musical smiles. In contrast, minor chords offer a more somber, introspective vibe, often bringing a touch of melancholy or tension to your tunes.

Seventh chords add another layer of complexity and richness to your music. By adding a fourth note to the basic triad, these chords create a fuller, more nuanced sound. They're the secret ingredient that can transform your song from good to unforgettable. You might recognize their sophisticated sound in jazz or blues, where seventh chords frequently enhance harmonic depth and emotional impact.

Chords evoke feelings and set the tone for your entire piece. As we've touched on, major chords often embody happiness or excitement, while minor chords can express sadness or longing. Let's say you're composing a song about a summer adventure—major chords might capture the joy and freedom you felt. Meanwhile, minor chords can underscore those feelings of loss and yearning if you're writing about the heartbreak of summer holiday love gone wrong.

To make your music resonate genuinely, you need to create compelling progressions of chords that form the backbone of your song. Many popular songs rely on tried-and-true progressions that instantly connect with listeners. One classic example is the I–V–vi–IV progression, used in hits like "Let It Be" by The Beatles, "With or Without You" by U2, and "Someone Like You" by Adele. This sequence creates a strong emotional pull and feels familiar to many listeners, so it's widely used. However, don't feel confined to these patterns—experimenting with unusual chord sequences can produce fresh, original sounds and help your music stand out.

Building tension and release within your progressions will keep your listeners engaged. Think of it like storytelling through sound

—introducing conflict with dissonant chords and resolving it with harmonious ones (5 *Essential Pop Chord Progressions and How to Use Them*). This ebb and flow of tension can evoke powerful emotions and make your song memorable.

Practical Exercise: Chord Progression Mapping

Grab your instrument and try mapping out different chord progressions. Start with something simple like C-G-Am-F, then experiment by swapping one chord for something unexpected. Play around with the order and see how it changes the mood of your music. You might stumble upon a progression that perfectly captures what you want to say.

Analyzing how popular songs use chords can also be enlightening. Listen closely to some of your favorite tracks and identify the chord progressions they employ. Notice how they fit into the song's overall structure and contribute to its emotional impact. You'll start recognizing patterns you can incorporate into your work.

The current example is "Shallow" by Lady Gaga and Bradley Cooper from the *A Star Is Born* soundtrack. The song uses the I–V–vi–IV progression in the verses, which gives it a strong, familiar emotional pull. This progression supports the song's themes of vulnerability and longing. As you listen, notice how the chords shape the mood and how the progression builds up to the more dramatic chorus. It's a great example of a simple progression that enhances the song's impact and connection with listeners.

Understanding chords and progressions is just one piece of the songwriting puzzle, but an essential one. It opens new creative avenues, allowing you to express yourself more fully through music. So, whether you're strumming on a guitar or tinkering on a keyboard, remember that every chord has its story to tell—how you string them together can turn an ordinary song into something extraordinary.

SCALES AND MELODIES THAT SPEAK

When you pick up your guitar or sit at the piano, creating a memorable melody starts with understanding musical scales. Scales are notes arranged in a specific order, providing the framework for your melodies. The two primary types are major and minor scales.

Major scales have a bright, happy sound and follow a specific pattern of whole and half steps. For example, the C major scale follows the pattern: C-D-E-F-G-A-B-C. A well-known song like "Twinkle, Twinkle, Little Star" is based on a significant scale.

Minor scales, on the other hand, often sound more somber or introspective. They follow a different pattern of intervals, typically with a more complex arrangement of whole and half steps. For example, the A minor scale follows the pattern: A-B-C-D-E-F-G-A. Minor scales commonly convey emotions like sadness or tension, adding depth and contrast to music.

Crafting memorable melodies becomes your next adventure once you have a grip on the scales. A catchy melody often has a precise melodic contour, meaning it has a shape or direction as it moves up and down. Think of it like drawing a line with your voice or instrument—each note adds to the picture. Repetition is key here. When your favorite song gets stuck in your head, it's usually due to its repetitive hooks. However, please don't overdo it; variation is also significant. Throw in some unexpected twists to keep things interesting. A melody with both repetition and variation keeps listeners engaged and wanting more.

Music isn't just about sound; it's also about feeling. Melodies can express many emotions—from joy to sorrow, excitement to nostalgia. Intervals—the distance between two notes—are essential in shaping this emotional expression. Small intervals, like seconds, create a sense of closeness or calmness, while larger ones can evoke drama or tension. A rising interval might suggest hope or anticipation, while a descending one could express resolve or reflection. Melody dynamics—how loud or soft you play—also contribute to the emotional impact. A quiet passage can draw listeners in, while a burst of volume can make them sit up and take notice.

Now, how do you weave these melodies into your songs? Start by synchronizing them with your lyrics and chords. Melody is the thread that ties everything together. Your lyrics carry the story, while the melody adds color and emotion. Create melodic hooks—short, catchy phrases that repeat throughout your song. These hooks are musical magnets, pulling listeners back to key moments in your piece—practice by singing your lyrics to different melodies and experimenting until you find the right combination.

HARMONIZING FOR DEPTH AND TEXTURE

Harmony adds richness and dimension to music by supporting the melody with additional notes or voices. It binds a song's elements together, transforming simple tunes into fuller, more emotionally resonant experiences. Think of a duet where both singers move together harmoniously; the result feels vibrant and complete. That's the power of harmony: not just an addition, but an essential part of a song's emotional and sonic depth.

There are various ways to create harmony. One common technique is parallel harmony, where two or more notes move in the same direction, maintaining a consistent interval. This creates a unified, blended sound that mirrors the melody while adding depth. Another approach uses countermelodies—independent melodic lines that weave around the main melody, offering contrast and complexity. These techniques can make a piece feel richer and more engaging.

Harmony is also shaped by genre. For example, in "Shallow" by Lady Gaga and Bradley Cooper, the harmonies in the chorus are intense and emotionally charged. Their voices blend to enhance the lyrical tension and make the song more impactful. In contrast, jazz compositions like "Take Five" by Dave Brubeck highlight harmony through unusual time signatures and complex chord progressions, creating a layered, exploratory sound.

Vocal harmonies bring an exceptional warmth and beauty to a song. Layering vocal parts can give the impression of a choir, even if only a few voices are involved. The key is balance—ensuring that each voice complements rather than overpowers the others. Artists like The Beatles and Pentatonix are known for their skillful vocal arrangements. Listening closely to their work can teach you how harmonies are structured and how different parts interact to create a cohesive whole.

To build your harmonic skills, spend time analyzing songs you enjoy. Focus on how harmonies are introduced—are they subtle background elements or do they take center stage? Notice how harmony is treated differently in various genres, from tight pop harmonies to jazz's experimental layers. This focused listening can deepen your understanding and inspire your musical creativity.

Whether through parallel lines, countermelodies, or layered vocals, harmony can elevate your music. It adds emotional weight, sonic interest, and a sense of completeness that draws listeners in and keeps them engaged.

RHYTHM AND GROOVE ESSENTIALS

Rhythm is the heartbeat of any song, providing the steady pulse that drives the music forward. It starts with the fundamental components of beat, tempo, and meter. The beat is the song's consistent pulse, while the tempo dictates how fast or slow the song moves. Meter organizes beats into repeating patterns, usually in groups of twos, threes, or fours. These elements help define the structure of the music, guiding the listener's movement through the song.

Creating an engaging groove goes beyond technical understanding; the goal is to create an emotional experience. A significant element is syncopation, where off-beats or unexpected parts of the measure are emphasized, adding unpredictability and keeping the rhythm lively. Different genres bring unique rhythmic styles, such as reggae's laid-back offbeat accents or hip-hop's intricate, percussive beats, each offering valuable insight into how rhythm can drive a song.

When songwriting, the rhythm should align with the lyrical flow to complement each other. Writing lyrics with a specific rhythm can enhance the connection between the words and the beat. To deepen your rhythmic vocabulary, try experimenting with polyrhythms—multiple independent rhythms played at once. Layering percussion elements, like hand claps or shakers, can also create a fuller sound, adding depth to the groove. Additionally, challenge yourself with rhythm-based songwriting exercises, like writing a piece where percussion takes the lead or creating a song that focuses solely on rhythmic elements, without relying on melody or harmony. These exercises will push your creative boundaries and expand your rhythmic range.

INTEGRATING RHYTHM, HARMONY, AND SONGWRITING

Mastering rhythm and groove opens the door to endless creative possibilities, making your music more engaging and dynamic. Harmony adds depth to your songs through subtle vocal harmonies or intricate countermelodies. Together, these elements transform simple ideas into captivating compositions. As you experiment with rhythm and harmony, you'll develop your unique voice, allowing you to craft songs that resonate with listeners long after they've heard them.

The next step is understanding how these elements combine structure and arrangement to create cohesive, purposeful songs. By honing these skills, you can write music that flows smoothly and leaves a lasting impact.

3

CRAFTING COMPELLING LYRICS

STORYTELLING THROUGH SONG

Lyrics can connect listeners to a song on a deeply emotional level. They tell stories, evoke imagery, and create personal connections. A well-crafted lyric can make a song relatable, memorable, and impactful. For songwriters, words function as a key storytelling tool, while the melody provides the framework that supports and enhances them. Understanding how to write resonating lyrics is essential to creating music that will leave a lasting impression.

Understanding narrative structure is essential in songwriting. Think of your song like a mini movie, with a beginning, middle, and end. The exposition sets the stage, introducing listeners to the world you're creating. It's where you lay the foundation, whether on a bustling city street or a quiet beach at sunset. Use vivid imagery to draw your listeners in, making them feel part of the scene. Next comes conflict or tension, an essential ingredient for engaging songs. It's the heartbeat of your story, the element that keeps listeners hooked. It's a relationship on the rocks or an internal struggle. Whatever it is, build it up gradually, weaving suspense into your lyrics. Finally, resolve the narrative arc effectively. This doesn't mean a successful conclusion; sometimes, leaving things open-ended or bittersweet can be more powerful. The main thing is to ensure your listeners feel satisfied after taking an emotional journey with you.

Creating relatable characters and themes is another layer of impactful storytelling. Characters don't have to be fleshed out like in novels, but they should feel real enough for listeners to connect. Start by building character profiles, jotting down their traits, desires, and flaws. Are they the high school rebels or the quiet dreamers? These details make them relatable (*How to Write Songs as a Teenager: 10 Steps (with Pictures)*). On the thematic front, explore universal themes like love, identity, and resilience. These threads weave through human experience, making your song relatable on a broad scale. When listeners hear your lyrics and think, "That's me," you'll know you've struck gold.

The verse-chorus format is a classic structure that enhances storytelling. Verses are where you develop your narrative—think of them as chapters in your storybook. Each verse should push the story forward and reveal new layers or perspectives. Choruses, on the other hand, are your story's anchor points. They encapsulate the song's core message or emotion, repeating it for impact. This repetition helps drive home your song's theme, making it memorable and resonant.

Incorporating dialogue and monologue within lyrics adds depth and dimension to your storytelling. Dialogue-driven verses can bring scenes to life, allowing listeners to eavesdrop on conversations between characters. It gives your song an almost cinematic feel, as if the listeners watch a scene unfolding before their eyes.

On the flip side, internal reflections in choruses offer insight into a character's mind or heart. These moments of introspection can be powerful, revealing vulnerabilities and desires that drive the narrative.

Reflection Exercise: Writing Your Story

Grab a notebook and pen. Think about a story you want to tell through song—maybe about a summer romance or overcoming a personal challenge. Sketch out a brief outline: What happened at the start? What conflict arises? How do things resolve? Next, jot down character details and themes you want to explore. Use this as a guide when writing your lyrics, ensuring your story unfolds naturally and engagingly.

Remember, storytelling in songwriting should involve words, emotion, and connection. When you write lyrics that tell a compelling story, you invite listeners into your world, allowing them to see it through your eyes. So, pick up that pen and start telling tales that captivate and inspire!

RHYME SCHEMES AND THEIR IMPACT

Lyrics dance to the rhythm of rhyme, each word carefully chosen to fit the melody. Rhyme schemes shape your song's flow, giving it structure and style. Let's explore different rhyme schemes and their effects on lyrical flow.

AABB, ABAB, and ABCB rhyme schemes each shape the flow and tone of your lyrics in distinct ways. AABB creates a straightforward, rhythmic feel by pairing lines that rhyme consecutively. ABAB introduces a back-and-forth structure, giving your verses a more dynamic and engaging quality. ABCB breaks the pattern slightly by leaving the second line unrhymed, adding an element of surprise that can make the lyrics more memorable and emotionally nuanced.

Internal rhymes are an effective technique for enhancing the rhythm and flow of your lyrics. They appear within a single line, adding energy and momentum to your phrasing. By creating unexpected moments of rhyme, they capture the listener's attention and keep the verse moving smoothly. While commonly used in hip-hop and rap for their fast-paced delivery, internal rhymes can elevate lyrics in any genre, turning straightforward lines into more engaging and dynamic expressions.

Balancing predictability with surprise in songwriting is a way to keep your audience engaged. Use rhyme to create familiarity, but don't be afraid to break patterns for emphasis. Deliberate disruption of rhyme schemes can add weight to specific lines, drawing attention to a key phrase or emotion. It's like a sudden pause in a conversation that makes everyone stop and listen. This technique can turn ordinary lyrics into something memorable.

Rhyme can amplify emotional resonance in your lyrics, giving weight to feelings and ideas. When you rhyme words at emotional peaks, you create moments that stick in the listener's mind. Rhythmic emphasis on main emotional words helps convey the intensity of your expression. It's like underlining a sentence or highlighting a phrase; it ensures the message hits home.

Now, let's get practical with exercises to experiment with different rhyme patterns. Start by writing a verse using a strict AABB scheme. Feel how the predictability anchors your lyrics. Next, rewrite it using an ABAB pattern, noticing how the alternation changes dynamically. Play with internal rhymes within these structures, adding complexity and rhythm. Once you're comfortable, try swapping rhyme schemes within a single song. Begin with AABB in the verses and switch to ABAB in the chorus. This exercise challenges you to think creatively and adapt your lyrics to different flows.

Constraint-based rhymes are another way to push your creative boundaries. Pick a word and challenge yourself to find as many rhymes as possible. Then, craft a verse with those rhymes as anchors (ASCAP). This forces you to think freely, finding new ways to express familiar ideas. It's an exercise in creativity and flexibility, two valuable skills for any songwriter.

Exploring rhyme schemes isn't just about following rules; it's about discovering how they can serve your song. Each scheme offers a different texture and mood, allowing you to tailor your lyrics to fit the emotion you want to convey. Whether crafting a heartfelt ballad or an upbeat anthem, understanding rhyme can help you communicate more effectively.

As you experiment with these techniques, remember that songwriting is an art form without strict boundaries. Rhyme schemes are tools meant to enhance your creativity, not constrain it. Find what works best for you and your music, and don't be afraid to break the mold when inspiration strikes. With practice and exploration, you'll develop a keen sense of how rhyme can transform your lyrics from ordinary lines into powerful verses that resonate deeply with listeners.

METAPHORS AND IMAGERY IN LYRICS

Metaphors and similes can make your lyrics hit harder and feel more real. A metaphor says one thing *is* another, like calling your heart a "lonely battlefield" to show emotional struggle without spelling it out. In Olivia Rodrigo's "Traitor," she sings, "You betrayed me/And I know that you'll never feel sorry," turning heartbreak into something almost physical.

A simile compares things using "like" or "as"—for example, "her smile is like sunshine." In Taylor Swift's "Red," she sings, "Loving him is like driving a new Maserati down a dead-end street," using a simile to describe fast, exciting love that leads nowhere. These devices let you say more with fewer words and help people picture your feelings.

Using imagery in your lyrics can pull listeners into your world. Think of describing a summer day so clearly that they can almost feel the heat or smell the ocean. You can practice this by writing about a moment using all five senses—what you see, hear, feel, taste, and smell. These details turn simple lyrics into something that feels real and unforgettable.

The mood of your song—the vibe—comes down to your word choices. Whether you want your song to feel chill, intense, or hopeful, the right words help set that tone. You can make it even more potent by tying in real experiences. Compare how something felt to a storm, a late-night drive, or anything that left a mark on you. That personal touch helps people hear your lyrics and feel them.

Poetic devices are like spices; they add flavor and depth to your lyrical stew. Personification, for instance, gives human traits to non-human elements, creating emotional depth. Imagine a moon that "whispers secrets" or a river that "sighs with longing." These lines breathe life into your words, making them resonate on an emotional level.

Symbolism is another way to add layers of meaning to your lyrics. It allows objects, actions, or themes to represent something more profound. For example, a red rose might symbolize love, while a broken mirror could represent shattered dreams. These symbols enrich your lyrics, allowing listeners to explore different interpretations. Take "The Climb" by Miley Cyrus—the idea of a "climb" symbolizes life's struggles and challenges. The climb represents personal growth, overcoming obstacles, and the journey to reach your goals, emphasizing that the journey is as important as the destination. Similarly, in "Chandelier" by Sia, the chandelier symbolizes reckless behavior and the self-destructive tendencies someone might use to cope with inner turmoil. It captures the conflict between excess and the aftermath of a chaotic life, offering a raw and intense portrayal of emotional struggle. These symbols add depth to the lyrics, creating a more engaging and reflective experience for the listener.

Integrating metaphors seamlessly into your song requires finesse. You want them to enhance, not disrupt, the flow of your lyrics. Blending literal and figurative language helps achieve this balance. Start with straightforward lines and weave in metaphors subtly, allowing them to complement rather than overshadow the overall message. Be mindful of clichés and overused metaphors—they can dilute the impact of your words. Instead, strive for originality, creating new expressions that surprise and engage.

Let's say you're writing about love. Instead of saying, "Love is a rose," which feels familiar and worn out, think about what love means to you personally. Perhaps to you, it's like a vine that grows stronger over time, wrapping itself around everything it touches. This fresh perspective adds authenticity and intrigue, capturing attention.

Metaphors and imagery are potent allies in crafting compelling lyrics. They invite listeners into worlds of wonder and emotion, transforming simple songs into unforgettable experiences. So, let your imagination run wild next time you write. Embrace the beauty of language and see where it takes you—your audience will thank you for it.

FINDING YOUR UNIQUE LYRICAL VOICE

Ever notice how every artist has a vibe that makes their work unmistakably theirs? That unique sound and style are what you want to find in your songwriting. Developing your lyrical voice is like discovering a hidden gem within yourself, waiting to shine. It starts with exploring your writing style, and there's no rush. This journey of self-discovery can be exciting and rewarding. Reflective journaling exercises can help you uncover what resonates with you. Spend a few minutes daily jotting down your thoughts, emotions, and experiences. Over time, you'll notice patterns and themes naturally occurring in your writing. These insights will lead you to your unique voice.

Analyzing your writing habits can also provide valuable clues. Are you drawn to certain themes, like love or adventure? Do specific words or phrases pop up repeatedly? Paying attention to these details helps you understand your creative inclinations. Your voice isn't something you create from scratch; it's an extension of who you are. So, embrace it, quirks and all.

Drawing inspiration from firsthand experiences adds authenticity to your lyrics. Your life is a treasure trove of material waiting to be tapped into. Consider personal milestones—first love, loss, triumphs, and failures. Each one carries a story worthy of being told. When you translate these experiences into universal themes, your music will resonate on a broader level. It's about finding the balance between the specific and the universal, making sure others can see themselves in your words.

Writing songs based on individual experiences invites listeners to step into your world and share your joy or pain. It creates a connection that goes beyond the notes and rhythms. Don't be afraid to be vulnerable; it's in those moments of honesty that true magic happens.

Balancing authenticity and creativity as you develop your lyrical voice is essential. Staying true to yourself doesn't mean sticking to one style or theme forever. It involves maintaining an authentic tone while allowing room for creative risk-taking. Experiment with different genres, styles, and structures. Push your boundaries and challenge yourself to try new things. Sometimes, stepping outside your comfort zone leads to surprising discoveries about your capabilities.

However, remember to stay authentic. Your audience can tell when you're faking it, so let your true self shine through your lyrics. Authenticity doesn't mean being genuine and relatable.

Consistency in voice is another important aspect of developing your unique style. It's like having a signature that people recognize instantly. Establish thematic coherence across your songs by weaving common threads through them. Perhaps it's a recurring theme or a particular way of expressing emotions. These elements will become part of your identity as an artist.

Creating a signature lyrical motif is another way to maintain consistency. This could be a specific phrase, style, or structure that becomes synonymous with your work. Think of it as a musical fingerprint that leaves an impression on everything you create.

As you explore these aspects of finding your unique lyrical voice, remember it's a continuous process. Your voice will evolve as you grow and change as a person and artist. Embrace this evolution and let it guide you toward new creative horizons.

In wrapping up this chapter, remember that your voice is the heart of your music. It's what makes your songs uniquely yours and connects them with others on a deeper level. As you progress, continue exploring and refining your style, drawing from first-hand experiences, and staying true to yourself while embracing creativity. With time and practice, you'll develop a voice that's unmistakably yours.

Next, we'll explore melody creation and how to craft tunes that perfectly complement your lyrics. Get ready to bring your words to life through music—let's make those lyrics sing!

4

HOOK TO HARMONY: UNLOCKING THE SECRETS OF SONGWRITING

CATCHY HOOKS THAT STICK

Hooks are one of the most essential parts of a song. They're the parts that get stuck in your head, make you want to sing along, and keep you coming back for more. A hook is usually a short, catchy phrase in the lyrics or melody that grabs attention fast and sticks with you long after the song ends.

What makes a hook so memorable? In most cases, it's all about simplicity. The easier it is to remember and repeat, the more likely it'll stay in your head. Think about the repeating "la la la" in Kylie Minogue's "Can't Get You Out of My Head", or the chill groove of "As It Was" by Harry Styles. Both songs use clear, simple ideas that are easy to grasp, and that's precisely what makes them work.

According to a study from the University of Wollongong (shared by *Neuroscience News*), hooks are even more critical today because of how music is listened to. Artists must grab attention quickly, as so many people are streaming songs and skipping between tracks.

A strong hook can make all the difference in getting listeners to stick around.

The genesis of hooks that linger involves designing melodies that strike a perfect equilibrium between simplicity and allure. One of the foundational techniques is repetition; reiterating a melody or lyric reinforces its presence in one's memory. However, beware of monotony's pitfall—overdoing repetition can transition a hook from sticky to stale. Thus, complement it with rhythmic diversity to maintain a sustained interest level among listeners. Even minor rhythmic shifts—a pause, an unexpected syncopation—can metamorphose a straightforward hook into something animated and enduring, ensuring it refreshes with every listen. Imagine the impact of building anticipation with a sudden pause followed by a rhythmic surge, subtly weaving complexity without compromising the melody's integrity.

Contrast is another secret weapon for making your hook stand out. Mixing things up—like jumping between high and low notes —can create tension and release that pulls listeners in. It's kind of like a musical rollercoaster that keeps your ears on edge in the best way. You can also play with changes in volume or speed. For example, dropping everything quietly before exploding into a loud chorus can be more complicated than staying loud the whole time.

Adding different instruments can also give your hooks extra flavor. A hook doesn't always have to be sung—sometimes a killer guitar riff or synth line can steal the show. Think about the intro of Olivia Rodrigo's *"good 4 u."* That angsty guitar riff kicks in, and you instantly know the song. It grabs attention and sets the mood before a single lyric is sung. And yeah, vocal hooks are great because they can show emotion in a way instruments can't—but don't sleep on instrumental hooks either. They can add layers, texture, and vibe, making the whole song feel richer and more exciting.

Interactive Exercise: Hook Creation Challenge

Try this engaging exercise to hone your hook-crafting prowess! Begin by selecting a simple phrase or melody—something straightforward yet full of potential. Then, immerse yourself in experimentation with various instruments to witness their transformation. Start with a keyboard, alter your approach with a guitar, and try out a digital beatmaker. Observe how each instrument infuses its character and mood into the hook. Upon discovering an arrangement that resonates with your vision, explore dynamics—manipulate tempo, alter pitch, and adjust volume to gauge how these elements impact the total auditory experience. By venturing through these musical corridors, you'll unearth innovative methods to etch your hooks into listeners' minds.

Hooks aren't just about making something catchy—they're the heart of your song; the part people can't stop singing. They're what sticks in someone's head long after the music ends. You can create hooks that stay with people by keeping things simple, repeating the right parts, using contrast, and playing with different sounds or instruments.

BALANCING MELODY AND LYRICS

The melody and lyrics must match the emotion and feel when writing a song. If the music doesn't fit the mood of the words, the message can get lost, like putting happy music behind a sad scene in a movie. The melody should support the story your lyrics are telling. For example, a rising melody can show excitement or hope, while a falling one can suggest sadness or calmness. This is called melodic phrasing, and it helps the listener feel the emotion behind the lyrics. When the shape of the melody follows the ups and downs of your lyrics, it makes your song feel more real and connected.

Consistency between melody and lyrics is another key element in songwriting. It ensures that your song feels cohesive from start to finish. Thematic coherence means your melody and lyrics should share a common thread: the mood or the message. It's tempting to throw in unexpected melodic twists, but too much can lead to dissonance with your lyrical themes, leaving listeners confused. Avoid jarring shifts that break the song's flow. Instead, maintain a unified emotional tone throughout. This consistency helps listeners stay engaged, providing a clear path for their emotional journey through your song.

Enhancing lyrical phrasing with melody involves using musical techniques to highlight important words or phrases. Melodic peaks—those high notes that stand out—can emphasize key ideas, drawing attention to peak moments in your lyrics. Think of singing about a special moment in your life; hitting a high note on the word "change" can underscore its significance. Similarly, pacing melodies to align with lyrical rhythm ensures that your words don't feel rushed or cramped. Let the melody breathe, allowing each word to resonate with its intended impact.

Experimenting with melodic rhythm opens new possibilities for supporting lyrical flow. Syncopation, which emphasizes off-beats, can add unexpected emphasis to certain lyrics, making them stand out. This rhythmic variation keeps listeners on their toes, maintaining interest throughout the song. Don't be afraid to vary rhythmic patterns within a song, allowing different sections to have a distinct feel while contributing to the overall narrative. This diversity adds texture and depth, creating a dynamic listening experience.

Understanding vocal range and type is fundamental when writing melodies that align with lyrical content and vocal capabilities. Knowing your vocal range will help you tailor melodies to suit your strengths, ensuring you can deliver them with confidence and expression. Each vocal type—whether soprano, alto, tenor, or bass—has unique characteristics that influence how melodies are crafted. Consider these qualities when composing; they can guide you in choosing pitches highlighting your voice's best features.

Improving and exercising your singing voice will unlock new levels—you have way more potential than you think. Regular practice is key, mainly when you include exercises that build range and flexibility. Vocal warm-ups are a must, kind of like stretching before a workout. Simple stuff like humming scales, lip trills, and sirens helps you safely explore your range and avoid strain. As you get more comfortable, try pushing beyond your usual notes—you'll open up new ways to express yourself. Learning to move smoothly between different parts of your voice, like chest and head voice, makes your singing sound more effortless and emotional. The more you practice, the more confident and versatile you'll become.

Utilizing vocal dynamics adds another layer of expression to your melodies. Crescendos—gradual increases in volume—and decrescendos—softening sounds—can heighten your song's emotional impact. For instance, a crescendo perfectly mirrors that growing anticipation if you're singing about building excitement. Dynamic contrast emphasizes key moments, drawing listeners' attention to specific phrases or sections.

Creating harmonies that resonate requires understanding the foundational elements of harmony creation. Intervals—the distance between two notes—carry emotional weight and define harmony's character (*StudySmarter*). Simple exercises can help you master basic harmonies using thirds and fifths as building blocks. Experimenting with close (notes near each other) and open (wider spacing) harmony will add texture to your songs.

Layering harmonies introduces depth by creating multiple vocal lines that blend seamlessly together. This layering enriches the overall soundscape while supporting melodic themes. Consider how different genres utilize harmony; pop music often features tight harmonies for catchy hooks, while folk music embraces open harmonies for warmth (*Full Voice Music*). Understanding these genre-specific techniques will allow you to adapt harmonies according to your artistic vision.

Incorporating harmonic movement keeps listeners engaged by ensuring the music evolves. Harmonic progressions that change subtly or dramatically maintain interest throughout the song's duration. Modulation—changing keys within a song—introduces variety, providing fresh perspectives on familiar themes (*Native Instruments*).

Balancing melody and lyrics involves careful consideration of emotional alignment, consistency, phrasing enhancement, rhythmic experimentation, vocal range adaptation, dynamic utilization, harmony building, and layering depth exploration across genres while maintaining movement within compositions, all contributing towards captivating crafting songs where words meet music harmoniously without missing beats!

EXPLORING VOCAL RANGES

Have you ever tried singing along to your favorite song only to find yourself straining to hit those high notes or struggling to reach the lows? This frustrating and all-too-common experience highlights the importance of understanding your vocal range. Awareness of your vocal range involves discovering your potential as a singer. Knowing your range will guide you through the vast and varied musical landscape, assisting you in avoiding those awkward moments where your voice refuses to cooperate with your aspirations. Instead of viewing it as a restriction or a limitation, consider it an opportunity to excel in areas where your voice naturally shines.

Identifying your vocal range involves discovering the lowest and highest notes you can comfortably sing, which might require experimentation and patience. This foundational knowledge becomes invaluable for writing melodies that suit your natural abilities. As mentioned, different vocal types, such as soprano, alto, tenor, and bass, have distinctive characteristics. Sopranos might find that they excel with soaring, exalted high notes that lift the listener to new heights, while basses provide the grounding with their deep, resonant tones that reverberate in the soul. By establishing which category you fall into, you open yourself up to exploring melodies that highlight these vocal qualities rather than creating unnecessary tension by working against them.

Crafting melodies that align perfectly with your vocal strengths involves staying within those comfortable pitch ranges. There's a big difference in writing a melody that gracefully sits within your voice's sweet spot—the notes naturally flow one into the other, and the transition feels as smooth as stepping through a familiar and well-worn path. This harmony between your voice and the melody makes singing an enjoyable experience, plus it enhances your song's emotional delivery. Your unique vocal qualities set you apart in these moments of perfect alignment. If you have a slight rasp, lucky you–consider it an asset and embrace it fully! Use this characteristic to add texture and heartfelt emotion to your melodies. Or maybe you have a flair for executing quick vocal runs or holding long, powerful notes. Creating melodies that allow these talents to flourish will make your music memorable and significantly impact your audience.

Utilizing dynamics in your melodies introduces complex layers of expression that mere words might struggle to convey. Imagine crescendos as the build-up to a musical climax, a gradual increase in volume that mirrors rising emotion or excitement, drawing the listener into your story. Conversely, decrescendos provide a gentle release, creating rich moments of intimacy or serenity that invite introspection. These dynamic shifts can transform a simple melody into an evocative emotional rollercoaster that engages the listener from start to finish. Dynamic contrast emphasizes certain parts of your song; for example, a sudden, unexpected dip in volume followed by an explosive rise can capture attention and keep listeners fully engaged. This technique is much like adding bold strokes to a canvas; it highlights what's essential and directs focus to where it truly matters.

Understanding how dynamics and transitions work provides the tools to shape your melodies to evoke genuine, deep-seated emotions from your audience. This understanding is the difference between merely singing words and making those words resonate, reaching deep into the listener's soul. By incorporating these techniques into your songwriting arsenal, you're doing more than creating music; you're crafting an experience that resonates on multiple levels, leaving an impression that people will return to repeatedly.

CREATING HARMONIES THAT RESONATE

Harmony in music is the combination of different sounds and notes that work together to create a fuller, richer experience. It involves creating a sonic background that supports the melody and makes the overall music more interesting, not merely stacking chords on top of one another. Harmony adds depth and emotion to your music, enhancing the listener's connection to the song.

To get started with harmony, you need to understand intervals— the distance between two notes. Each interval creates a different mood. Smaller intervals can create tension, while larger intervals tend to feel more open and resolved. For example, a third interval (two notes three steps apart) has a warm, pleasant sound, while a seventh interval can feel unresolved, leaving the listener wanting more. Playing or singing two notes and listening closely can help you hear how different intervals affect the sound.

Once you're comfortable with intervals, you can start layering harmonies to add more depth to your music. Harmonies are the extra notes you sing or play alongside the melody to make it fuller. For instance, singing a third above your melody will create a smooth, consonant sound, while a fifth adds stability and power. Depending on your desired sound, you can experiment with close harmonies (where the notes are close together) and open harmonies (where the notes are further apart). Each type of harmony brings a different feeling, intimate or grand.

The way harmony is used changes depending on the music genre. In pop music, harmonies are often used to elevate the chorus, making it feel more powerful and uplifting. In folk music, harmonies tend to be more natural and simpler, helping to tell a story rather than focusing on technical perfection. Listening to different genres and paying attention to how artists use harmony can give you new ideas for your music.

Movement in harmony is essential to keep your listeners engaged. Harmonic progressions, or how chords change throughout a song, should evolve to maintain interest. You can start with simple chords and gradually add variation by substituting chords or changing keys unexpectedly. This will keep your music fresh and dynamic.

Another way to add excitement is through modulation, changing the song's key. Modulating can give the song a new energy or shift the mood, helping to keep the listener's attention.

Creating harmony is a way to express emotion and create an experience for your listeners. You can craft music that feels deeper and more engaging by understanding intervals, layering harmonies, and using movement and modulation. In the next chapter, we'll explore how these elements form a complete song structure, helping you create songs that flow smoothly and effectively tell a story.

5

SONG STRUCTURE AND ARRANGEMENT

THE ANATOMY OF A SONG

Songwriting is an art that blends creativity, imagination, and technique. Each part of a song—verses, choruses, and bridges —plays a vital role in shaping the overall piece, much like the tools and materials used to build something functional and meaningful. Each section serves a unique purpose and adds something meaningful to the overall story and emotion you want to express.

Let's break down the main parts of a song. Verses are where the story starts to unfold. They provide context and background, giving listeners essential information about the song's theme. This is where you introduce the "who," "what," and "where," setting the stage for everything that follows. The chorus is where the main message or theme of the song comes into play. It's the catchiest part that sticks with listeners and communicates the heart of your music in a simple, memorable way.

Next, the bridge adds something different to the song—either a change in perspective or a shift in mood. This part helps keep the listener's attention, like a plot twist in a book that keeps things interesting. A well-crafted bridge can change the song's vibe and make the return to the chorus feel even more powerful.

Putting these parts together correctly is essential to making your song engaging. The sequence in which the verses, chorus, and bridge appear will affect the song's emotional impact, guiding your listeners through feelings. Pacing matters should keep the listener interested without dragging on or feeling rushed. Think of it like the rhythm of a good conversation, where each point naturally flows to the next.

Song structures act as guidelines for organizing your ideas. For example, the AABA structure features verses, a bridge, and a final verse, creating a build-up and a satisfying conclusion without overusing repetition. The ABAB format, where verses alternate with choruses, gives listeners a balanced flow between familiar and new sections. The ABCB structure adds variety by introducing a new section, keeping the song dynamic and preventing it from becoming too predictable.

Let's look at some successful examples in more detail. Take, for instance, a pop anthem like Katy Perry's "Firework," which utilizes a verse-pre-chorus-chorus structure to deftly build momentum and deliver its empowering message (*Understanding the Most Common Song Structures*). This structure effectively channels emotion and uplifts listeners, creating a resonant anthem. Alternatively, explore indie music's experimental and evocative side with songs like Bon Iver's "Holocene," which boldly defies traditional structures while still creating an evocative and profoundly moving soundscape.

Exercise: Dissecting Song Structures

Now, we invite you to grab your favorite song and dissect it. Analyze its structure meticulously. Identify the verses, choruses, bridges, and other emerging sections. How do they contribute to the song's overall flow and emotional impact? Notice how each part serves the song's story and emotional arc, much like individual scenes in a movie contribute to the overarching narrative. This engaging exercise will sharpen your analytical skills and deepen your understanding of effective songwriting techniques.

Understanding these components and their interaction will allow you to create songs that resonate deeply with listeners. Whether you stick to classic structures that have stood the test of time or dare to venture into experimental realms, remember that each artistic choice shapes your song's unique journey. You are inviting others to step into your world through the powerful and transformative medium of music.

VERSE-CHORUS DYNAMICS

In songwriting, moving from the verse to the chorus is like shifting gears in a car—it must be smooth and well-timed. One way to do this is by adding a pre-chorus, which acts like a bridge, gently easing the listener from the verse into the energy of the chorus. The pre-chorus helps build excitement, increasing emotional tension and preparing everyone for the big moment in the chorus. Another cool trick is modulation, changing the song's key to make the shift even more powerful. This shift can give the chorus a fresh burst of energy and make it feel like the song has peaked.

To make sure your verse and chorus feel different, make each section stand out. You can change the melody, maybe keeping the verse calm and soft, and then turning the chorus up with a more energetic, bold melody. This contrast helps make the song feel like it's telling a story, where the verses share the details, and the chorus gives you the emotional punch. You can also switch up the lyrics between these sections. Maybe the verses are reflective, and the chorus is about confidence or celebration. This contrast adds layers and makes the song more engaging.

Writing a great chorus is a skill on its own. Repetition is super important here—repeating specific phrases or melodies makes them stick in the listener's head. But don't just repeat it for the sake of it. Mix some rhythm changes or syncopation (a little rhythm surprise) to keep it fresh and interesting. These little twists will help your chorus stand out and stay catchy.

The verses are where you tell your song's story. Use them to dive deeper into the narrative, adding detail and meaning. This is your chance to build up tension and set the stage for the emotional release in the chorus. Think of the verses like chapters in a book, revealing more of the story with every line, and leading into the powerful chorus.

You'll make songs that connect with listeners when you combine all these elements—smooth transitions, contrast between sections, catchy choruses, and detailed verses. Whether you're writing a chart-topping pop hit or an emotional indie track, these techniques will help your music hit harder emotionally and leave a lasting impression. Don't be afraid to experiment and find what works for you. Songwriting isn't a one-size-fits-all thing; it's about exploring and making your sound your own. Keep practicing; over time, you'll develop your style and sense of what makes each song memorable.

BRIDGES AND BEYOND

Your song flows smoothly, but it needs something to shake things up. That's where a bridge comes into a section that brings a fresh twist or shift, like a sudden surprise that changes the story's direction. It gives your song a break from the usual and adds something unexpected, whether a change in mood, lyrics, or melody. A good bridge amps up the excitement and keeps things interesting when the song might feel predictable. It's your chance to show off your creativity and take your listeners somewhere new.

But don't stop there—think about other ways to add depth to your song. An intro, whether a chill piano part or a high-energy guitar riff, sets the vibe. It pulls listeners in and gives them a sense of what's to come. Then, the outro is like your song's final statement, leaving a lasting impression. Adding an instrumental break or solo lets the instruments have their moment to shine and gives the song a little breathing space before diving back into the next section.

Changing things up throughout your song is essential to keep people hooked. You can surprise your listeners with tempo shifts, like speeding things up or slowing them down to create a dramatic change. You can also switch keys to change the emotional vibe, making it feel fresh. Layering different instruments—like adding strings for a smooth touch or electronic beats for a modern feel— gives the song more texture and makes it stand out.

Sometimes, breaking away from the usual song structure can lead to excellent results. Experiment with unique structures like free-form songs that flow without strict rules, or through-composed tracks that tell a continuous story without repeating sections. Progressive rock or electronic songs might evolve as they go, taking listeners on a constantly changing journey. These structures help your music feel fresh and exciting, pushing boundaries and making your track unforgettable.

A song might start with a slow, building intro that leads into verses telling a story of change. The bridge shifts the mood and tempo when the listeners think they know where it's headed. After that, an instrumental break highlights superb guitar solos before bursting into the chorus with a new burst of energy. Finally, the outro wraps everything up, leaving a strong, emotional finish.

Bridges and additional sections are what elevate your song and keep it dynamic. They create contrasts and build excitement, ensuring your song stays fresh and engaging from start to finish. By experimenting with these elements, you can craft something unique that resonates with your audience.

Think about blending different styles or genres within these sections. Mixing classical strings with electronic beats for an unexpected twist or adding a jazz solo to an indie rock song for a cool, sophisticated vibe can make your song stand out. There are no rules—only opportunities to explore and make something new.

With each decision, you shape your song's personality and how it impacts listeners. Don't be afraid to take risks and make your song stand out! Let bridges become more than just transitions—let them transform your song into an unforgettable musical experience. There's endless potential to experiment and express yourself, so dare to be different.

ARRANGING FOR MAXIMUM IMPACT

You've probably already nailed the melody and lyrics when crafting a song, but something still feels off. There's one missing piece: the arrangement. Arranging your song involves combining the instruments and vocals to create something that grabs people's attention and makes them feel something. Carefully blending elements that complement one another creates a cohesive and engaging sound.

THE POWER OF VOCALS

Start with your vocals, which are the core of your song. Adding layers of harmonies helps build on a foundation. Each harmony can add emotional depth, like a choir that supports the main vocal, making the song feel bigger and more impactful. Backing vocals can echo important lines or create a call-and-response effect, making the song even more dynamic. These subtle layers help draw the listener in and keep their attention, giving your song a fuller, richer sound.

HARNESSING DYNAMICS

Next, think about dynamics. This involves using changes in volume to control the song's emotional flow – you're adjusting the emotional intensity with a volume knob. Using volume swells, where the sound builds and fades, can make moments feel more dramatic, while crescendos (gradual increases in volume) and decrescendos (gradual decreases in volume) guide the listener through the song's emotional highs and lows. These shifts give the song life, syncing with the lyrics and creating an atmosphere that reflects the feelings you want to express.

STORYTELLING THROUGH ARRANGEMENT

Arranging your song goes beyond just sound—it's a way to tell a story. How you arrange your instruments can highlight the emotions and themes of the song. For example, you could use a piano motif that repeats throughout the song, representing a character's journey or internal struggle. Changing the pacing at different points in the song can also help tell the story, slowing things down before a big emotional moment builds anticipation. When you align your arrangement with the song's narrative, it makes the song more impactful and gives listeners a deeper connection to what you're saying.

EXPERIMENTATION AND INDIVIDUALITY

This is where things get exciting: experimenting with different techniques to make your song stand out. With all the tools available today, you can try out loops, samples, or even remix an existing song to create something new. Pushing boundaries and exploring what works for your unique sound lets you turn an acoustic song into an electronic banger or reimagine a track in a completely different genre. Explore and figure out what fits your identity as an artist!

CRAFTING THE PERFECT ARRANGEMENT

A song isn't just a bunch of parts thrown together; it's a carefully arranged story, from start to finish. By understanding how instruments and dynamics work together, using storytelling to guide your arrangement, and experimenting with new techniques, you can create something that grabs the listener. The challenge is to find the right balance between being creative and keeping the structure intact, so that every element of your arrangement serves the song's message.

Arranging your song for maximum impact is essential to take your music to the next level. Every choice you make in the arrangement affects how the song feels and how it connects with your audience.

You have the power to create something unforgettable, something that sticks with your listeners long after the song ends.

As we wrap up this chapter on song structure and arrangement, keep these techniques in mind and use them to write songs that are as unique and personal as you are. In the next chapter, we'll look at songwriting technology and explore how modern tools can help you amplify your creativity and connect with listeners worldwide. Get ready to take your songwriting to new heights!

6

CONNECTING EMOTIONALLY
WITH YOUR AUDIENCE

WRITING WITH EMOTIONAL INTELLIGENCE

You're chilling in your room, headphones on, letting the music take over. The song hits you in a way that feels like the artist just read your mind and turned your emotions into music. It's that magic moment when the song speaks directly to you, and you feel understood. That connection is the heart of emotional intelligence in songwriting. It goes beyond writing lyrics—it's about crafting stories and experiences that connect with people on an emotional level.

Start by thinking about what emotions hit you the hardest. What makes you feel super happy, sad, or even mad? Understanding what triggers those feelings helps you write lyrics that are true to your feelings. For example, a minor key can capture sadness, while an upbeat, fast tempo can make you feel pumped and joyful. Knowing how your audience will think is just as important. When you write with empathy, you're not just singing at them; you're having a conversation, creating an emotional bond.

Turning your emotions into music is where the fun begins. Let's say you want to express hope—how would you do that in a song? You might use an uplifting primary key or an energetic tempo to evoke those positive vibes. But if you're writing about heartbreak, a slower beat with sad, minor chords could express that feeling better. These musical choices help you create the vibe you want to share with your listeners. The more you experiment with different sounds, the more you determine what works best for the emotions you want to convey.

Thinking about how your audience will feel is key to writing songs that resonate with everyone. Universal emotions like love, loss, and hope are things people worldwide experience, and they'll connect with your music on a deep level. When writing, try to put yourself in the shoes of the people who will hear it. What are they feeling? How can your song amplify those feelings and help them process their emotions? This will help create a shared experience that feels personal to your listeners.

To make your song feel alive, think about layering instruments and using dynamics (changes in volume) to make the emotion pop. Picture your song as a journey through different moods—each instrument you add brings something new to the vibe. Strings might create a soft, romantic feel, while drums bring energy and movement. Changing the volume, like going from soft to loud, adds intensity and mirrors how emotions shift throughout the song.

Reflection Exercise: Emotional Mapping

Please take a moment to immerse yourself in one of your favorite songs and map out the emotions it evokes. Focus intently and note how the song influences your feelings at various points throughout. Which distinct musical elements contribute to these emotions? Are there notable shifts in tempo, rhythm, or dynamic changes? Employ this reflective exercise to understand how emotions are deeply connected to music and apply these insights to enrich your songwriting process.

Writing with emotional intelligence means creating profound connections that transcend the barrier of words. It involves composing music that speaks directly to the heart, making those rare and indescribable moments where listeners feel understood and recognized. So, the next time you sit down to write, remember that this incredible power of connection lies entirely in your hands —or rather, within the reach of your voice and the strings of your instrument.

EVOKING EMOTION THROUGH MUSIC

When you're at the piano, each note you play isn't just a sound but a feeling waiting to be shared. Music speaks the language of emotions, and elements like melody, harmony, rhythm, and dynamics are your way of expressing those feelings. The rise and fall of a melody—called melodic contour—carries emotions just like someone's voice. A soaring melody might show hope or deter-mination, while a gentle drop could make someone feel reflective or nostalgic. These shifts in the melody can create a bond with anyone listening.

Harmony helps add depth to your music's emotional story. Think of it like the emotional push and pull you feel in life. When you build tension with chords, you can make listeners feel anticipa-tion or unease; when those chords resolve, it brings relief. The balance between tension and release mirrors life's emotional rollercoaster. Playing with these elements lets your music become more than just something people hear—it's something they can feel.

However, it's not just about notes and chords. Music also has emotional signals that help guide the listener's experience. Modulation, for example, is like shifting gears in a car. Changing the key in the middle of a song can signal a shift in mood or perspective, giving your song a new emotional direction. Rhythm also plays a considerable role—think about how a fast, steady beat might make people feel confident or determined, while unpredictable rhythms can create excitement or surprise.

Try to find the right balance between musical complexity and emotional clarity. You don't always need a complicated arrangement. Sometimes, a simple melody gets the emotional point across perfectly. These simple melodies let listeners connect without feeling overwhelmed. If you make things too complex, the emotion might get lost, and the listeners could feel disconnected.

Also, don't be afraid to experiment with sounds that aren't typical. Experiment with adding sound effects like rain or distant thunder to create mood. These extra layers can give your music texture and evoke different feelings. And trying out unusual instruments can open more emotional possibilities, like a theremin, which can bring a creepy vibe, or a ukulele, which adds a fun, light-hearted touch.

BUILDING AN EMOTIONAL ARC

Generating an emotional arc in music involves defining an emotional trajectory that seamlessly guides listeners from one feeling to another. Start by outlining the emotional journey you want your song to take. Where does it begin emotionally? What are the high points? Where does it leave the listener by the end? Sad? Satisfied? Or disquieted? Crafting these peaks and valleys creates an engaging narrative that keeps listeners invested.

Song structure supports this emotional flow. Building tension in verses and releasing it in choruses creates contrast and highlights emotional shifts. As we've seen, bridges offer a perfect opportunity for an emotional shift—a moment of reflection or revelation before returning to familiar themes. These structural elements help guide the listener through your song's story, ensuring each section contributes to the overall emotional impact.

Creating tension and release is an art that, if mastered, keeps listeners on the edge of their seats. Crescendos, those gradual buildups of sound, lead to climactic moments that resonate deeply. Dynamic contrasts—shifts from soft to loud or slow to fast—highlight emotional changes and add excitement to your music. These techniques create an immersive listening experience that fully engages all emotions.

Guiding listeners through an experience involves more than just telling a story; it's about creating a cohesive emotional journey. Narrative techniques such as pacing changes reflect emotional progression throughout the song. A slower pace might convey introspection or longing, while quickening rhythms could capture urgency or joy. By thoughtfully arranging these elements, you'll create an experience that will resonate long after the music has ended.

AUTHENTICITY IN SONGWRITING

Embracing authenticity in songwriting means finding and expressing your authentic voice without fear of imitation. Your voice is unique—an amalgamation of your experiences, thoughts, and feelings—and deserves to be heard. Journaling exercises help you explore this voice by reflecting on firsthand experiences and emotions. Writing from personal experience adds authenticity to your lyrics, making them relatable and genuine.

Steer clear of copying others! Skip the clichés and focus on being original. Following trends or mimicking popular artists is tempting, but real creativity comes from finding your style. Think about the experiences that have shaped who you are and use them to tell your story in your songs. For example, if you've been through a tough breakup, instead of writing the same "heartbreak song" you've heard a million times, dig into what happened—how it made you feel, what you learned, and how you grew from it. Or maybe you've faced significant challenges in school or with friends. Instead of using overused phrases, write about how those struggles changed you and what you now know about yourself or others. These personal stories will make your lyrics feel real and relatable, setting you apart from the crowd.

Connecting authentically with the audience requires vulnerability —sharing personal truths through your music. Relating these personal moments to universal themes allows listeners to see themselves in your songs, forging a connection that transcends superficial boundaries. By staying true to yourself and embracing authenticity in songwriting, you'll create music that touches hearts and leaves an impression without needing flashy gimmicks or trends.

As we wrap up this chapter on emotional connection and authenticity, remember to let your music reflect who you are, what you've been through, and how you view the world. Let your authenticity shine through every chord and every word, creating an emotional bond with those who listen. In the next chapter, we will explore those dreaded creative blocks.

7

OVERCOMING CREATIVE BLOCKS

SPOTTING WHAT'S BLOCKING YOUR CREATIVITY

E ver stare at a blank page or your instrument, waiting for an idea to show up ... and nothing happens? It happens to all of us. Creative blocks are fundamental; the first step to getting past them is knowing what's causing them. Much of the time, it's not just that you don't have an idea, it's the fear that your song won't be good enough or that people won't get it. That pressure can mess with your head and make you second-guess everything. If you're worried about what others will think or comparing yourself to other musicians, that fear can shut down your creativity before you start.

One helpful way to figure out your creative patterns is to keep a journal—not the "dear diary" kind, but something simple to jot down when you feel the most innovative. Was it after a late-night jam with friends? After a walk in nature with your earbuds out? When you know what gets your ideas flowing, you can plan your writing time around that. Some days, your brain's not in the zone, and that's okay. But if you know your peak times, you can make the most of them and enjoy the process instead of forcing it.

Your space matters too. If your room or practice area is a total mess, it might be harder to think clearly. A chilled, organized space can help you focus and let your ideas breathe. And don't forget the pressure from people around you, sometimes expectations from friends, family, or even social media can make you feel like you must be perfect. That kind of pressure can block your creativity. When you notice what's throwing you off—your environment or outside pressure—you can start changing those things and create a vibe that supports your music.

Practicing mindfulness might sound kind of out there, but it helps. Taking a few minutes to slow down and breathe can clear your mind and help you refocus. When your brain is full of random thoughts, doing something like deep breathing or even short meditation can help you feel grounded. It's like clearing out a messy room in your mind so you can find the good ideas hiding in the clutter. Learning to be present—just focusing on *right now*— can open the door to fresh inspiration and new creative energy.

Reflection Exercise: Uncovering Your Creative Patterns

Start a notebook—or even a note on your phone—where you can track your creative process. Write down what gets your ideas flowing: Is it late-night playlists? Doodling in class? Chilling in your favorite spot? Figuring out what lights that spark helps you tap into your creativity more easily and often.

Getting past creative blocks doesn't mean you'll never face them; it means learning how to handle them without getting overwhelmed. Sometimes, you hit a wall because you're out of ideas or worried your work won't be strong enough. When you notice those patterns, like through journaling, you start to understand what's holding you back and how to move forward.

BREAKING THROUGH WRITER'S BLOCK

Writer's block can feel like an uninvited guest that overstays its welcome, but there are ways to kick it out. Engaging in creative prompts and exercises can reignite that spark. Try random word association games: grab a dictionary, pick a word, and let it lead you somewhere unexpected. Or indulge in freewriting sessions where judgment is left at the door— write whatever comes to mind. Let your thoughts spill out without worrying if they make sense. Musical improvisation challenges are also an excellent way to break free. Grab your instrument, set a ten-minute timer, and play whatever you feel. Don't worry about perfecting it; just let the music guide you.

Sometimes, shaking things up with a new perspective can help clear the creative cobwebs. Write a song from a different point of view—imagine being in someone else's shoes for a moment. How do they see the world? What stories would they tell? Collaborating with other songwriters can also offer fresh insights. Bounce ideas off one another, and you might find inspiration in places you never thought to look. Sometimes, seeing things in a new light helps.

Physical activity is another ally in the fight against creative stagnation. Movement can free up mental space and get those creative juices flowing again. Go for a walk or a jog and let your mind wander. The rhythm of your steps might match your next song's beat. Dancing is a way to release pent-up energy and open new channels of creativity. As you move, feel the music, and let it lead you wherever it wants.

Exploring new musical genres and styles can breathe fresh air into your songwriting. Step out of your comfort zone and dive into sounds you wouldn't usually listen to. Try spinning some traditional West African drumming, Native American flute music, or the hypnotic tones of the Australian didgeridoo. You could even pick up an instrument you've never played—like a kalimba (thumb piano) or a guzheng (a Chinese string instrument). These unique sounds can trigger unexpected ideas and give your music a new vibe. Sometimes, the key to unlocking creativity lies in embracing the unfamiliar and letting it inspire you to create something original.

When writer's block strikes, it's tempting to think creativity has abandoned you. But remember, it's always there—sometimes, it just needs a little nudge to come out and play. Whether trying random word games, shifting perspectives, moving your body, or exploring new musical styles, these strategies can help you break through those blocks and find your creative groove again.

Remember that writer's block is not permanent; it's more like a passing cloud obscuring the sun momentarily. With patience and persistence, you can find your way back to that place where ideas flow freely and songwriting feels like second nature again. So next time you're staring at that blank page, try one of these techniques and see what happens. You never know where inspiration might lead you next.

CULTIVATING A CONSISTENT WRITING ROUTINE

Building a solid songwriting routine can boost your creativity. One way to stay consistent is by setting specific times to write. Some people like to try "morning pages"—a simple habit where you jot down whatever's on your mind right after waking up. It helps clear mental clutter and gives your creativity a jumpstart for the day. If you're not a morning person, find a time that fits your schedule better, like during a quiet evening or after school. Whether you write every day or a few times a week, having a regular schedule trains your brain to get into creative mode more easily.

Having a dedicated space to write can also make a huge difference. Set up a corner of your room as your songwriting zone—somewhere that feels comfortable and inspires you. Keep it tidy and distraction-free so you can focus. Add things that motivate you, like posters of your favorite artists, cool lighting, or anything else that sparks good vibes. When it's time to write, silence your phone and let others know you're in your creative zone.

It also helps to have someone to keep you motivated. Try teaming up with a friend who writes songs too—you can share your work, give feedback, and keep each other on track. If you don't have a songwriting buddy nearby, join online songwriting groups or challenges to connect with people who are into the same thing. Having a supportive crew makes it easier to stay committed.

Don't forget to celebrate your wins, no matter how small. Finishing a verse, figuring out a strict rhyme, or recording a rough draft are all steps forward. Reward yourself with something you enjoy, like a break, a snack, or your favorite playlist. Keep track of your progress in a journal or voice memos—it's a great way to look back and see how far you've come whenever you're feeling stuck.

Interactive Element: Songwriting Goal Tracker

Create a simple chart or table where you can track your songwriting goals. Include columns for the date, specific goal (e.g., write two verses), and a checkmark for completion. This visual representation motivates and is a tangible reminder of your progress.

Establishing a consistent writing routine might initially feel tough, but it becomes second nature with time and commitment. By establishing designated times for creativity and building an environment that supports regular writing, you're laying the groundwork for sustained success. Incorporating accountability mechanisms keeps you motivated, while celebrating milestones ensures you recognize and appreciate each step forward. You'll create a rhythm that feels as natural as breathing—one where creativity thrives without pressure or strain. So, whether it's morning pages or late-night sessions, find what works for you and watch your songwriting journey unfold with newfound consistency and joy.

EMBRACING IMPERFECTION

Perfectionism can sneak up on you like that voice that never stops pointing out what's "wrong" with your music. One tiny mistake, one lyric that doesn't sound quite right—suddenly, you feel like scrapping the whole thing. That voice might tell you to rewrite and rewrite until every note is "perfect." However, chasing perfection can kill your creativity. Instead of making progress, you get stuck second-guessing yourself and never finish anything.

Your first draft must not be perfect—it just must exist. It's like the rough version of a sketch: it gives you something to shape and improve later. Permit yourself to mess up. Every mistake teaches you something, and each one brings you closer to your real sound and style.

Try shifting your mindset from needing everything to be flawless to appreciating the steps you're taking along the way. Every verse you write or melody you figure out is progress. A song doesn't have to be polished to have power—sometimes those rough edges make it even more meaningful. For example, a shaky vocal take might capture more emotion than a super-clean one. Or that weird guitar riff you made by accident? It could be the most unique part of your track. These imperfect moments are sometimes what make a song stick with people.

Think about how live performances feel different from studio recordings: they're raw, emotional, and energetic, even if they're not technically perfect. That kind of realness is what people connect with.

It's also important to be kind to yourself during the process. Talk to yourself the way you'd talk to a friend. If you mess up, don't beat yourself up—remind yourself that creating music takes practice, patience, and time. Say things like, "I'm learning with every song I write," or "My music doesn't have to be perfect to matter." Keep a journal to track your progress and remind yourself how far you've come, even if it's just finishing a chorus or recording a new idea.

Ultimately, songwriting isn't about being flawless; it's about being real. Letting go of perfection allows your creativity to flow and helps your songs sound more honest and emotional. Your music becomes more than just notes and words; it reflects you, genuine, evolving, and perfectly imperfect.

As we wrap up this section on creative blocks, remember that imperfection often makes music unforgettable. In the next chapter, we'll explore how these ideas play out when co-writing with others, blending your voice with someone else's to create something amazing together.

8

ANALYZING SUCCESSFUL SONGS

DISSECTING CHART-TOPPING HITS

Imagine sitting in your room, earbuds in, and that one song plays. You know the one—it's beat makes you nod, its lyrics feel like they were written just for you, and before you know it, you're hitting *replay*. Why does this song have such power over you? Let's focus on what makes these hits resonate so widely.

At the core of every hit song are elements that connect with listeners fundamentally. It's like baking a cake—skip the sugar, and you miss the sweetness. Catchy hooks and memorable melodies are the sugar in your musical recipe. These components stick in your mind like gum on a shoe, making them unforgettable. Think of hooks as your song's business card. They introduce you to listeners and leave an impression after the music fades.

Universal themes with emotional appeal also play a massive role. Songs that tackle love, heartbreak, or self-discovery tap into our shared feelings. This connection creates a bond between the artist and the audience, making the song feel personal yet widely relatable.

Now, let's talk structure—how songs are built to keep us hooked from start to finish. Successful songs often use well-crafted build-ups and breakdowns, creating a dynamic flow that engages listeners. These elements act like waves, lifting you and bringing you back down to create an emotional journey. Instrumental solos or breaks are strategically placed to provide breathers, keeping the song interesting without overwhelming the listeners. This balance of tension and release is key to maintaining momentum.

Next up in our dissection is production—the unseen yet essential ingredient that elevates a song from good to great. It's the polish that makes every note shine. The layering of instruments and vocals adds depth and texture, creating a rich soundscape that envelops listeners. Effects like reverb and delay can introduce atmosphere, adding a sense of space and mood. Think of singing in your bathroom versus an open field; the acoustics change how you experience sound. Producers use these techniques to create immersive audio experiences that captivate audiences.

But what keeps you coming back for more? Audience engagement is the secret sauce here. Successful songs use tempo changes strategically to surprise listeners and maintain interest. A sudden shift in speed can jolt you awake, while a slowdown invites introspection. Songs with elements like call-and-response encourage participation, turning listeners into active participants rather than passive consumers. It's like being at a concert where the crowd sings; everyone becomes part of the magic.

Interactive Element: Song Analysis Checklist

To apply these insights to your songwriting, try this activity: Pick a favorite hit song and analyze its components. Identify the catchy hook, note the song's structure (verse-chorus-bridge), and evaluate the production techniques used. Consider how tempo changes or audience interaction elements are woven into the music. Use this checklist to dissect what makes your chosen song tick.

GENRE VARIATIONS AND THEIR ELEMENTS

Let's explore the world of musical genres. Each genre feels like its own universe, with unique rules and characteristics that define its sound. Take blues, for instance. It's built around the 12-bar blues progression—a simple yet powerful sequence forming countless songs' backbone. This progression gives the blues its signature feel, transporting listeners to a place of raw emotion and story-telling. It's not just music; it's also history, carrying tales of struggle and resilience.

Flip the record to hip-hop, and you'll find a different landscape. Here, lyrical flow and rhythm reign supreme. Words spill out like water from a faucet, each line written with precision and flair. The genre thrives on its ability to weave intricate stories through rap, creating a dynamic interplay between words and rhythm. It's a dance of language where every syllable counts.

Then there's country music, where storytelling takes center stage. It's like listening to an audiobook set to music with each song unfolding like a short story. Country artists are experts in narrative depth, drawing listeners in with tales of love, loss, and life on the open road. They make you think of a dusty highway stretching out ahead, the radio playing songs that speak to the heart of human experience. Country captures these moments and makes every story feel personal and honest.

In today's music scene, genres often blend like colors on an artist's palette. This cross-genre fusion has created exciting new sounds that defy traditional boundaries. Rock and electronic music have merged to create high-energy tracks that pulse intensely. It's the type of music you'll hear at a festival, lights flashing as the music pumps through massive speakers. It's an electrifying experience where rock's raw energy meets electronics' polished precision. Meanwhile, pop has borrowed elements from reggae, adding a laid-back groove to its catchy hooks.

Music doesn't exist in a vacuum. Its cultural and historical contexts shape it, and these infuse genres with meaning and significance. Jazz, for example, has deep roots in African American history, emerging from communities that used music as a form of expression and resistance. Close your eyes and listen to a jazz performance; it's like stepping back in time, and you can feel history's echoes in every note. Similarly, reggae has been a massive part of many social movements, its rhythms carrying messages of unity, justice, and change.

Genres don't stay static; they evolve in response to cultural shifts and technological advancements. Classic rock gave way to indie rock as artists sought new ways to express themselves. Electronic music has also transformed from ambient soundscapes to the high-energy beats of EDM that pack dance floors worldwide.

Understanding these genre variations helps songwriters appreciate the richness of music and find inspiration in unexpected places. Whether you're drawn to country's heartfelt narratives or hip-hop's rhythmic complexities, each genre enriches your creative process. As you explore these elements, remember that genres are not boxes but starting points for innovation. Embrace the diversity of sounds available to you and let them inspire your songwriting journey.

LESSONS FROM LEGENDARY SONGWRITERS

These musicians might not be from your generation, but their impact on music is undeniable, and their songwriting techniques are still worth learning today. Artists like Bob Dylan, Joni Mitchell, Paul McCartney, and others created songs that shaped entire eras, yet their lyrics, melodies, and creative processes continue to influence musicians across all genres. They're classics not because they're old, but because their work still connects, inspires, and teaches us something new, whether you're just picking up a guitar or writing your first lyrics.

Take Bob Dylan, for example. Known for his gravelly voice and powerful lyrics, he used songwriting to comment on the world around him. In songs like *"Blowin' in the Wind,"* Dylan tackled significant issues like war, peace, and freedom using meaningful but straightforward words. He didn't just write to rhyme—he wrote to make people think. His genius was turning complex ideas into lyrics that felt poetic and honest, inspiring generations to see music as a tool for change.

Then there's Joni Mitchell. When she wrote songs like *"A Case of You,"* she wasn't just writing lyrics—she was telling deeply personal stories. Mitchell's songs often come straight from her life and are filled with emotion and honesty. Her writing style is like journaling in song form, with vivid details and raw feelings that make listeners feel right there with her. That's her magic: she makes her personal experiences feel universal so anyone can relate.

Paul McCartney, one of the Beatles, is known for writing iconic melodies that people still sing today, like *"Hey Jude"* and *"Let It Be."*

Many of those tunes came to him in everyday moments. He once said that the melody for *"Yesterday"* came to him in a dream. McCartney often sat down at a piano or with a guitar, played around until something clicked, and followed his gut. His process shows how powerful spontaneity and trusting your instincts can be when creating.

Carole King took a collaborative approach. In real sessions with other musicians—like when she co-wrote *"You've Got a Friend"*— she thrived on teamwork. She was part of a community of writers at the famous Brill Building in New York, where ideas bounced from one person to another. Her strength was blending different voices and styles into something unified and heartfelt. Her career proves that songwriting doesn't have to be a solo act—some of the best songs come from shared creativity.

In interviews, Bruce Springsteen talked about how he finds inspiration in regular life—walking through his neighborhood, talking to friends, or observing people. His songs are often based on these small, everyday moments. For him, songwriting involves paying close attention and turning what you see and feel into music.

Stevie Nicks, from Fleetwood Mac, has described how lyrics sometimes just "come to her" out of nowhere. She'll hear a line in her head and write it down before it disappears. She trusts those flashes of inspiration mean something, and she follows them. Her experience shows that songwriting can sometimes be about listening to your thoughts, emotions, or dreams, and being brave enough to go where they lead.

You can also learn from someone like Leonard Cohen, whose songs read like poems. His lyrics are packed with meaning, carefully crafted word by word. His storytelling pulls you in, making you feel like you're on a journey with him. Try building a whole story into your songs with a beginning, middle, and end—to make your music more powerful.

And today, artists like Taylor Swift carry on these traditions. Swift uses her real-life experience, friendships, heartbreaks, and personal growth to turn them into deeply relatable songs. She shows that your story is worth telling and that honesty in your music can help others feel understood.

All these artists found their way to express themselves, and you can too. Their techniques aren't just part of music history; they're tools you can use today. Whether you're writing alone, jamming with friends, or pulling ideas from your everyday life, you're stepping into the same creative space they did. Let their methods inspire you, but make your voice your own.

APPLYING SUCCESS TO YOUR SONGS

So, you've taken a deep dive into some of the most successful songs. Now what? It's time to transform all those insights into your musical creations. Start by adapting song structures that fit your style. Maybe you've noticed that a particular structure, like a verse-chorus-bridge format, resonates with you. Try playing around with it. Adjust the length of verses or add an extra bridge to twist your song. Remember, structure is your friend, not a limitation.

Melodies are another area where you can let your creativity run wild. Think about those catchy tunes that stick in your head long after you've heard them. What makes them so memorable? Is it a particular melodic pattern or a surprising note that catches you off guard? Experience these elements in your music. Twist them, turn them on their head, and see what happens. The goal isn't to copy but to find what works for you and make it your own.

Don't hesitate to mix things up with techniques borrowed from successful songs. Blending genres can create a fresh soundscape that stands out. Try combining the storytelling depth of country with the rhythmic intensity of hip-hop. The result? Perhaps a unique blend that tells a story in a way only you can. Unexpected chord progressions offer another avenue for exploration. Maybe throw in a minor chord where listeners expect a major one, adding tension and intrigue to your song.

Building a personal songwriting toolkit can help you keep track of all these innovative ideas. Start by creating a library of hooks and lyrical ideas. Jot them down whenever inspiration strikes, whether you're sitting in class or waiting for the bus. Over time, you'll have a collection of gems ready to polish into full-fledged songs. Developing a repertoire of chord progressions is also essential. These progressions are like the backbone of your songs, providing structure and support. Experiment with different combinations and note how they affect the mood and tone of your music.

Self-reflection is key to growth, especially in songwriting. Take time to journal your discoveries—what worked, what didn't, and why. Write down how specific techniques influence your creative process or how blending genres opens new doors for expression. You might be surprised by the patterns that emerge over time, offering insights into your style and evolution as a songwriter.

Recording and reviewing song drafts can also provide valuable feedback for improvement. Listen to your recordings with a critical ear, noting areas for enhancement or modification. Perhaps the melody lacks impact, or the lyrics need tweaking for clarity. These observations will guide you in refining your craft, turning rough drafts into polished pieces perfect for sharing.

In reflecting on these techniques and their impact on your songwriting journey, remember that growth is an ongoing process.

Whether successful or not, each experiment will teach you something valuable about yourself as an artist. Embrace the challenges and triumphs, knowing they shape who you are becoming musically.

As we wrap up this chapter on applying success to your songs, remember that every step forward is progress. These insights from analyzing successful music are tools to help build your unique voice in songwriting. Our next chapter will explore collaboration and how working with others can further enhance creativity and innovation. So, open yourself up to new possibilities through shared musical experiences!

9

EXPLORING MUSICAL DIVERSITY

GENRE EXPLORATION AND EXPERIMENTATION

You might not have grown up with rows of vinyl records or classical concert halls, but today's music scene was built on a foundation of genres that have shaped how we listen and create. From the raw energy of rock to the smooth flow of jazz and the elegance of classical, each genre has its own vibe and set of defining traits. Rock is driven by loud guitars, steady drum beats, and a rebellious attitude—it's been the heartbeat of garage bands, music festivals, and wild road trips for decades. Jazz stands out with its improvisation and swing, where musicians bounce ideas off one another in real time. It is unpredictable, emotional, and full of expression. Classical music brings structure and complexity, with rich arrangements designed to take listeners on a journey— no words needed.

Today, many artists are mixing genres to create new sounds that push boundaries. Think of Billie Eilish blending pop with dark, minimalist electronic beats or Lil Nas X combining country elements with hip-hop in *Old Town Road*. These are not random pairings—they are intentional choices that show how combining genres can lead to something bold and original. Try using a folk-style guitar riff over a trap beat, or singing R&B vocals over indie rock chords. These creative fusions can make your music stand out and reflect who *you* are as an artist.

To tap into this creative mix, start by figuring out which genres you connect with the most. What music gets you hyped? What lyrics hit the hardest? Try making a "genre board"—like a vision board for music. Add screenshots of album covers, playlists, artists you admire, and sounds you want to try. This will help you see your influences and may inspire your style.

An excellent way to experiment with genre is through covers and mashups. Take a hit pop song and slow it down into a jazz version, or give an acoustic ballad a hip-hop twist. These reworks sharpen your musical skills and open your mind to what's possible when genres collide. Blending genres allows you to invent something entirely your own, whether in your bedroom with a laptop or at band practice with friends.

Interactive Exercise: Genre Mashup Challenge

Try this: Pick two or three genres at random—say, rock, jazz, and electronic dance music. Choose a popular song from each genre and listen closely to its defining characteristics. Then, challenge yourself to create a mashup using elements from each one. How does incorporating rock's powerful guitar riffs enhance jazz's melodic improvisation? What happens when electronic beats support them both? Document your process and reflect on what worked well, what didn't, and what surprised you. This exercise encourages experimentation without boundaries.

Exploring musical diversity through genre experimentation is like opening doors to new worlds. Each genre offers tools and textures waiting for you to discover. By embracing this diversity in your songwriting journey, you'll expand your horizons and experience music in ways you never have before.

CULTURAL INFLUENCES ON SONGWRITING

You do not have to travel far to explore the rich sounds of global music traditions—they influence artists worldwide and can inspire your songwriting too. Take African drumming, for example. These rhythms have been passed down through generations and are a form of communication and storytelling. Each pattern holds cultural meaning, often tied to ceremonies, daily life, or community events. The pulse and energy of these drums can bring raw emotion and intensity to music, which is why so many modern genres, from hip-hop to EDM, have roots in African rhythm.

Similarly, Indian classical ragas offer a deep well of inspiration. A raga is not just a scale—it is a framework that combines specific notes with rules for using them to express different emotions, times of day, or even seasons. Musicians spend years studying how to play and interpret ragas because every note matters and carries feeling. These melodies are often slow-building and full of detail, making them excellent tools for adding emotional depth and uniqueness to your music.

By studying these traditions and listening to how they are used in different songs today, you can experiment with adding global influences to your work. Whether layering a West African drum groove into a pop beat or building a melody that draws on the emotional range of a raga, these cultural elements can give your music a personal voice yet deeply connected to the broader world.

Latin American rhythms also provide a vibrant palette awaiting your exploration. Styles such as salsa, samba, or cumbia embody lively beats and infectious energy, igniting an irresistible urge to move. By blending these rhythms into your songs, you can revive your music, infusing it with warmth and vitality. These cultural elements invite listeners to experience the vibrant joy and passion inherently present in Latin music traditions.

Furthermore, stories and myths from various cultures can serve as a deep well of inspiration for your songwriting themes. Folklore narratives are laden with rich imagery and timeless teachings that echo across different societies. Try crafting lyrics that narrate the saga of a mythological hero's quest or a legendary creature's journey. These tales offer boundless possibilities for metaphorical exploration, allowing you to channel complex emotions through universally relatable narratives. Cultural motifs present a treasure trove of lyrical metaphors. Consider symbols like the phoenix emerging from ashes or the lotus blooming in muddy waters—each represents transformation and unwavering resilience. They can infuse your lyrics with layers of meaning, inviting listeners to delve deeper into the stories you tell through your music.

Instruments originating from diverse cultures can broaden your musical toolkit. The sitar, with its distinctive, resonant twang, instantly conjures the essence of Indian music. Its melodious sounds can infuse an exotic touch to your compositions, transporting listeners to lands pulsating with color and sound. Likewise, the didgeridoo offers atmospheric effects capable of transforming a song's mood entirely. Its resonant drone creates an otherworldly ambiance that captivates and intrigues audiences.

As you explore diverse cultural sounds and styles, take some time to think about your background, too. Your culture, family traditions, and personal history can be a powerful part of your songwriting. Writing songs about your heritage—like a family story, a holiday you celebrate, or something unique to your community—can make your music feel more real and meaningful. These personal touches will let people connect with your songs on a deeper level and help you share who you are with your audience.

If you are inspired by music from cultures that are not your own, that is impressive—make sure you approach it respectfully. Rather than simply using interesting sounds or styles, focus on understanding where those elements come from and what they represent. Take time to learn, attend cultural events, listen to traditional artists, and talk to people from those communities if possible. The more you understand, the more thoughtful and creative your music will be.

As you continue your songwriting journey, remember that inspiration can come from all corners of the world. Exploring music beyond your usual playlists and embracing global sounds, stories, and traditions opens the door to fresh ideas and deeper creativity. Whether it's the heartbeat of African drums, the emotion of Indian ragas, or the energy of Latin rhythms, these influences can add richness and meaning to your music. Blending your own experiences with cultural elements will help you create songs that are personal yet powerful enough to connect people across backgrounds.

FUSION AND INNOVATION IN SONGWRITING

You can create something entirely by mixing old-school sounds with modern styles. For example, combining the emotional storytelling of folk music with the energy of electronic beats is a growing trend among emerging artists. The raw strum of an acoustic guitar can be layered over a deep, pulsing synth to produce a sound that feels nostalgic yet new. Even a banjo paired with a heavy bass drop has been used successfully in genre-blending tracks. These unexpected combos can help you develop a sound that stands out and reflects your style.

Another direction to explore is mixing jazz with hip-hop. Jazz brings creative freedom, complex chords, and unpredictable rhythms—all of which can add depth to your beats. Artists have used smooth saxophone loops under rap verses or played with jazzy rhythms in drum patterns to create rich, layered tracks. This approach will expand your musical skills and bring a fresh edge to your sound.

And do not forget—technology is your creative sidekick. Today's digital tools allow you to turn regular sounds into unique effects or new textures. Vocal editing software can create ghost-like echoes or robotic tones, while sampling lets you pull sounds from all kinds of music, like old jazz records or traditional instruments from around the world. These samples can become the core of new tracks and give your music a global, one-of-a-kind feel. By blending tradition with innovation, you can make your songs meaningful, memorable, and entirely.

Breaking traditional songwriting boundaries invites you to explore new territories without constraints. Why stick to fixed song structures? Experiment with songs that defy typical formats, letting the music dictate its path. Atonal or microtonal scales offer further possibilities for innovation. These scales deviate from standard Western tuning and create unfamiliar yet intriguing sounds. They challenge listeners' expectations and invite them into a world where music doesn't follow predictable patterns. This approach requires bravery and an open mind, but can result in compositions that stand out in their originality.

Collaboration is another key to innovation in songwriting. Collaborating with artists from different musical backgrounds brings fresh perspectives and ideas that enrich the creative process. Try co-writing sessions where each participant brings unique influences—an electronic producer, an indie guitarist, a classical violinist—each adding their voice to the mix. The result is a mix of sound created from diverse streams of experience and style. These collaborations provide opportunities for mutual growth and discovery.

Through fusion and innovation, you have the power to redefine what music can be—an expression of your individuality and a reflection of the world around you. In these moments of creativity, where genres blur and boundaries dissolve, you'll find your voice that resonates with authenticity and originality in every note and rhythm.

EMBRACING GLOBAL MUSIC TRENDS

Scrolling through a playlist today, you'll probably find energetic beats from Tokyo, smooth rhythms from Rio de Janeiro, and calming melodies from Mumbai. The global music scene is more diverse than ever, with influences from every corner of the world. Staying updated on international music trends is a way to keep your playlists fresh and helps you stay connected to the broader music culture. By following international music charts, you'll gain insights into the sounds and styles resonating globally, giving you a window into the shifting musical landscape. Platforms like Spotify and Apple Music provide curated global playlists, allowing you to access a variety of genres and influences easily. Listening to these tracks broadens your musical perspective and deepens your understanding of the diverse, dynamic world of music today.

Bringing some of these world music elements into your songs can make your music stand out. For example, try adding Afrobeat rhythms to your tracks—they are energetic and make people want to move. These complex rhythms and basslines can turn a simple song into a total dance anthem. Or you could use reggaeton's catchy beats in a dance track for a fun and upbeat vibe that is perfect for any party playlist. Adding global influences like these can give your music a fresh sound that captures people's attention and keeps them hooked.

Writing music for a global audience means being inclusive and thoughtful about your lyrics. Try writing a few lines or a chorus in a different language to connect with listeners from other cultures. It does not have to be a whole song—you intend to embrace diversity and tap into themes everyone can relate to, like love, hope, or resilience. These themes cross cultural boundaries and connect us all on a human level, no matter where we are from. By focusing on what we all share, your music can reach a wider audience and leave a lasting impact.

Look at successful global collaborations to get ideas for your music. For example, Despacito became a massive hit by mixing reggaeton with pop and featuring artists from diverse backgrounds. It shows how blending styles can create something that resonates with listeners worldwide. You can also learn a lot from global music festivals, where assorted styles and cultures come together to celebrate music's unifying power. These events show how music can bring people from all occupations together, and by studying them, you can find inspiration for your projects.

As we wrap up this chapter, remember that exploring global music trends opens endless creative expression and connection opportunities. Your music has the power to speak to people all over the world, creating bonds that go beyond borders. In the next chapter, we will dive into how storytelling techniques can level your songwriting, helping you craft songs that captivate listeners and leave an impression.

10

FEEDBACK AND GROWTH

THE ART OF RECEIVING FEEDBACK GRACIOUSLY

You are sitting in your room, headphones on, fully immersed in the soundscape of your latest creation. Each beat, melody, and lyric has been carefully crafted and represents a musical effort and an extension of your innermost thoughts and feelings. Now, it is time to share this piece of your work with friends who can give you the feedback you need. Their expressions may shift from concentration to joy, curiosity, or confusion as they listen. Each look they give offers valuable feedback, helping guide your artistry's growth. They can direct you toward necessary improvements that might not have been obvious.

The feedback you get provides a fresh, objective perspective and reveals details in your work that you might have missed. As creators, we can become attached to our ideas, making it difficult to see areas for improvement. Feedback helps us view our work through new eyes, highlighting aspects that need adjustment. However, not all feedback is equally valuable. It can range from constructive advice to responses that may not be helpful. Sifting through these diverse types of feedback is necessary to improve your work.

Approaching feedback with an open mind is essential. It's instinctive to guard your creation protectively, but sometimes, that makes it harder to objectively evaluate the feedback you receive. However, if you can, embracing suggestions with a willingness to accept alternatives enlarges your horizon and keeps personal biases at bay. Try not to see it as criticism. Transforming feedback into a learning opportunity elevates it into a powerful growth asset.

Managing negative feedback can initially feel daunting and even distressing. It's easy to take personal offense or to become disheartened. However, sustainable artistic growth thrives on resilience. When critique feels too harsh or seems unwarranted, practice the art of active listening. Actively seek to understand the feedback by asking clarifying questions—showing you're enthusiastic about improvement, committed to the dialogue, and interested in growth. This approach also indicates maturity and open-mindedness, which will fortify your creative journey. Consider the feedback a chance to identify areas ripe for improvement rather than fixating on negatives. Even the world's greatest artists have all, at some point, weathered unfavorable reviews.

Transforming feedback into actionable goals is a strategy essential for ongoing development. Start by making a comprehensive feedback action plan. Dissect each piece of advice into achievable milestones, putting your finger on specific targets to be aimed for with each rework. Documenting each step will clarify the path forward and allow you to measure progress, savoring each improvement and acknowledging feedback's role in propelling your capabilities forward. Gradually, as your abilities grow and your talent deepens, your self-assurance as an artist will likewise swell. Constructive feedback is a propulsion that can push you toward a brighter artistic future.

Interactive Element: Feedback Reflection Exercise

Pause to contemplate the feedback you have recently received. Take a moment to write down the primary insights from this feedback session. Thoughtfully consider how to fuse these insights into your next creative project and produce specific, actionable steps for enhancing different facets of your work. By setting precise goals based on the advice and outlining detailed steps for assimilating this knowledge into your project, you can ensure that each critique serves as a stepping stone to a broader, more impactful evolution in your musical journey.

BUILDING A SUPPORTIVE CREATIVE COMMUNITY

Creative communities are your musical family. These groups are places where you can grow and find inspiration. They're where you can share your wildest ideas without fear of judgment. Explore local music clubs or online forums for young musicians to find the right community. These spaces are bustling with people who share your passion for music. You might see a local club that hosts open mic nights or a forum where songwriters exchange tips and advice. Participating in music workshops or meetups is another fantastic way to connect with like-minded individuals. Here, you'll learn new techniques, gain insight into different perspectives, and even find a mentor or two who can guide you on your artistic path.

Once you've found your community, it's time to foster collaboration and mutual support. Co-writing sessions with peers can be enriching. When you write with others, you blend unique styles and ideas, creating something unique that none of you could have made alone. It's fun to sit in a circle with friends, each armed with a guitar or a keyboard, tossing ideas back and forth until something clicks. Group critique sessions are equally beneficial as they offer a space to share your work and receive constructive feedback. These sessions often lead to shared learning experiences, allowing everyone involved to grow and improve together.

Being part of a community also means contributing positively. Offering constructive feedback to others is a great way to help them grow while also honing your critical listening skills. When you give feedback, focus on what works well in their music and supportively suggest areas for improvement. Sharing resources and opportunities is another way to contribute. If you come across a music competition or an open mic event, share it with your community. Your generosity could help someone else step forward in their musical career.

Building long-term creative relationships requires effort and dedication, but the rewards are immense. Networking at events and festivals is a good way to start. These gatherings are filled with people who are just as enthusiastic about music as you are. When you attend these events, don't be shy about introducing yourself and striking up conversations. You never know who you might meet—a future collaborator, a mentor, or a lifelong friend. Once you've made these connections, try to maintain regular communication. Whether through emails, social media, or the occasional coffee meetup, staying in touch with your peers will strengthen the relationship.

Interactive Element: Community Contribution Challenge

Here's a challenge: Commit to contributing positively to your creative community at least once a week for the next month. This could be by offering feedback on someone's song, sharing an opportunity you've found, or organizing a small group jam session. Track your actions and how they impact you and your community members.

ITERATION AND IMPROVEMENT

You've probably realized by now that songwriting isn't a one-and-done deal; it is a continuously evolving process. Initially, you start with a rough, unpolished idea full of endless possibilities. Each draft you painstakingly write provides an opportunity to express your artistic vision. Through each iteration, you discover nuances of expression that are uniquely yours. Every rendition of your song acts as a snapshot, encapsulating your skills, thoughts, and emotions at that precise moment in time. Making multiple drafts allows you to explore diverse musical ideas without pressure to get everything right on your first attempt.

Through this exploratory process, you can experiment with varying tempos, create shifts in dynamics, or let your creativity guide you to transform a verse into a chorus—or, in a more adventurous twist, turn a chorus into a bridge. Let your inspiration lead you down uncharted paths where flipping the bridge on its head might bring unexpected harmony to your creation. You never know which intricate combination of elements will resonate deeply with your audience until you dare to evaluate it. Indeed, songwriting is all about finding the right balance.

Applying feedback is where your song can truly blossom and take its whole form. Once you have gathered insightful observations from various listeners, it is time to identify recurring themes woven throughout their comments. It could be the case that numerous people pinpoint a specific lyric that feels slightly off, or the consensus might suggest the melody requires a spark of energy or excitement. These frequently mentioned points are your guiding stars, directing you toward refining and perfecting your work. Making such adjustments might mean rewriting significant parts of your melody or thoughtfully tweaking your lyrics to better capture and convey the underlying emotions for which you are aiming.

Keeping track of your progress is one of the best ways to see how far you have come—and to figure out where you want to go next. That is where a songwriting journal can come in handy. It works like a personal log of your creative journey, helping you capture random ideas, note changes you have made, and record significant breakthroughs. Write down what worked, what did not, and how specific feedback helped you improve a song's flow or vibe. Reviewing your old notes or drafts will show how your sound and skills have evolved.

Setting clear goals helps you stay focused and motivated. Try creating a checklist based on what you want to improve. That might mean getting better at writing strong hooks, learning how to structure your verses more clearly, or trying out styles you have not explored yet. You stay organized and make steady progress by breaking those goals into smaller steps and setting realistic deadlines. Instead of rushing the process, you build consistent momentum and give yourself time to grow naturally. Each small win moves you closer to the kind of artist you want to become.

Songwriting is a cycle of experimenting, refining, and learning. Every version of a song offers a chance to evaluate innovative ideas and push your creative limits. Change is part of the process.

The more you revisit, revise, and reflect, the more original and honest your music will become.

CONFIDENCE IN SHARING YOUR MUSIC

Sharing your music with others can be intense. When you put your songs out into the world, it can feel like everyone is watching and listening closely, and that kind of exposure can make you feel vulnerable. It is normal to feel nervous or doubt yourself during this process. That is why it is essential to remind yourself why you started making music in the first place. Your voice and perspective are unique, and your songs reflect your identity. When self-doubt creeps in, challenge it with tangible, positive reminders: instead of thinking "I'm not good enough," try "My music reflects who I am, and someone out there will connect with it." These thoughts build confidence and help you move forward even when fear shows up.

Performing in front of people can be nerve-wracking, but it is also one of the best ways to connect with listeners. Preparing for an open mic, school showcase, or any live gig involves more than just practicing your set—it also means mentally preparing. Visualizing a robust performance and focusing on your progress can help ease your nerves. When you step on stage, remember that your music gives people a glimpse into your world. You are not just playing a song but also sharing your experiences, thoughts, and feelings. Audience reactions can vary; sometimes, you get unexpected or unwanted feedback. Instead of letting that throw you off, try to learn from it. Please pay attention to what is useful and use it to improve, while letting go of anything that is not constructive.

Social media and music platforms make it easier than ever to share your work and build an audience. Creating an online presence is a smart way to get your songs out there and connect with other musicians and fans. You can post short clips, behind-the-scenes content, or livestream your songwriting process to let people in on your journey. Platforms like SoundCloud, YouTube, and Bandcamp are perfect for uploading full tracks and getting feedback from people worldwide. These tools give you access to listeners you might never meet in person—and each upload is a step toward building your musical presence.

Success in music does not just come from writing perfect songs—it comes from growing, learning, and staying open to new experiences. Celebrate every win, even the small ones. Take time to recognize your progress, whether it is a nice comment, a new follower, or a solid live performance. Reviewing what worked and what could be better helps you stay sharp and keep improving. Setbacks are part of the journey, too. Every time you push through a tough moment, you get stronger and more prepared for what is next.

As this chapter wraps up, remember that confidence does not happen overnight—it builds with practice and persistence. Sharing your music is a bold and creative move that helps you grow as an artist and connect with others meaningfully. Whether performing live or posting online, each step you take shapes your path. Keep going, and trust that every experience adds something valuable to your journey. The next chapter will explore how technology can take your songwriting to the next level.

11

SONGWRITING WITH TECHNOLOGY

DIGITAL TOOLS FOR SONGWRITERS

You are in your room, strumming your guitar, and a great melody comes to you—but your notebook's nowhere in sight. This is when technology steps up. Digital tools are changing how music is made, making it easier to capture, shape, and share your ideas from anywhere.

One of the most potent tools in music creation today is a Digital Audio Workstation (DAW). Programs like GarageBand and Ableton Live are excellent places to start. GarageBand is perfect for beginners—it is user-friendly and comes with virtual instruments, so you can build full songs without needing a full band. If you are into electronic music or enjoy looping and live remixing, Ableton Live offers more advanced features and real-time tools that DJs and producers love (*Best DAWs for Beginners in 2023*).

Writing lyrics can be tough, especially when you are stuck on a line or cannot find the right rhyme. Apps like MasterWriter help with that by giving you a massive database of rhymes, synonyms, phrases, and even pop culture references. It is like having a lyric coach on your phone.

When ideas hit at random moments—whether at school, outside, or just walking around—voice memo apps can help you record them quickly before they slip away. Got a cool melody or lyric line? Just pull out your phone and hit *record*. If you want to start building beats on the go, try BeatMaker. It lets you create drums and rhythms from your phone or tablet, turning spare moments into creative sessions.

Virtual instruments and plugins are the way to take your sound to the next level. You can add electronic synths, new textures, and realistic instrument sounds without expensive gear. Synth plugins give you access to many custom sounds, while drum machines help you build tight rhythms that make your songs hit harder.

Collaboration is another area where technology is changing the game. Tools like Splice let you upload your projects, grab samples, and work with producers worldwide. Want to make a song with a friend who lives in another state? Soundtrap lets you do that in real-time. It is a cloud-based studio where you and your collaborators can record, edit, and mix tracks, even if you are miles apart.

These tools make it easier to stay creative and connected and push your music forward—anytime, anywhere.

Interactive Exercise: Tech Toolkit Checklist

Create a "Tech Toolkit Checklist" for your songwriting journey. List the digital tools you want to explore—like DAWs, mobile apps, and virtual instruments—and note what each one offers. This will keep you organized and help you plan which tools to try next in your creative process.

In this digital age, technology is a powerful ally for songwriters looking to explore new horizons and push creative boundaries. Whether you're recording a melody on the go or collaborating with a friend across the globe, these tools can help bring your musical visions to life. They're gateways to endless creativity. Embrace them, experiment with them, and watch how they transform the way you make music.

HOME RECORDING BASICS

Setting up your home studio is like building a creative nest where your musical ideas can take flight. Finding the right space is crucial. You'll want a room that doesn't echo like a cave or sound like a train station. Look for a quiet, calm spot, a bedroom corner, or a basement nook. Pay attention to the acoustics—hard floors and bare walls can cause sound to bounce unpredictably. Arranging furniture, hanging thick curtains, or adding rugs can help tame the sound. You want to create an environment that supports creativity and makes you comfortable.

Next up, gear up with the basics. A good microphone is your voice's best friend, capturing every nuance and emotion you pour into your music. You don't need to break the bank; there are fantastic budget options that deliver quality sound. Pair it with an audio interface, which bridges your mic and computer, ensuring clear signal transfer. Don't forget headphones. They're necessary for accurate monitoring, allowing you to hear every detail without outside interference. All these elements work together to bring your home studio to life.

Understanding signal flow is key to making your recordings shine. Think of it as water flowing through pipes from a tap to a glass; you want it to be smooth and uninterrupted. Start by setting up your signal chain: connect your mic to the audio interface and then the interface to your computer. This clear path will ensure your recordings are crisp and free from unwanted noise. When recording vocals, focus on technique. Maintain a consistent distance from the mic and stay aware of plosives (like 'p' sounds) that can distort recordings. For instruments, experiment with mic placement. Angle the mic differently to capture various tones and textures.

Creating the perfect recording environment involves more than just plugging in equipment. Acoustic panels are lifesavers in reducing unwanted noise and reflections. They absorb echoes and keep your recordings clean. Positioning them strategically around your space will ensure optimal sound capture. When setting up microphones, consider their placement relative to your sound source. Experiment with distance and angle to find the sweet spot that captures the essence of your performance.

Once you've laid down your tracks, it's time to polish them into a masterpiece. Editing and mixing give your songs that professional touch. Start with basic EQ (equalization) to balance frequencies and ensure clarity. Remove any muddiness by cutting lower frequencies and enhancing the midrange for vocals and instruments. Compression helps control dynamic range, smoothing out peaks and bringing quieter elements forward.

Adding reverb and delay introduces depth and space to your mix. Reverb creates the illusion of room size, making vocals sound like they're in an intimate hall or an expansive arena. Delay adds an echo effect, creating layers and dimension within your track without overwhelming it. Use these effects sparingly—they should enhance, not overshadow.

Recording at home offers freedom unparalleled by studio constraints. It's about creating a space to experiment, make mistakes, learn, and grow as an artist. Each recording session is a stepping stone in developing your unique sound and style.

Quick Tip: DIY Acoustic Panel

Try making your own acoustic panel to clean up your recording sound without spending much. You only need a simple wooden frame (about 2 ' x4'), some rock wool or Owens Corning 703 insulation, and a layer of breathable fabric like burlap or cotton. Build the frame, stuff it with insulation, and wrap it tightly with the fabric using a staple gun. Then hang it on your wall or lean it in a corner where sound tends to bounce. It's a cheap, effective way to reduce echo and improve your recordings—and you can even customize it with cool fabric to match your room's style.

USING TECHNOLOGY TO ENHANCE CREATIVITY

Have you ever found yourself stuck with the same chords or melody, feeling trapped in a loop of sameness? Well, maybe that's not such a bad thing. In music, looping and sampling can be game changers. Creating loops for different song sections is a good way to experiment with structure. Try writing a catchy chorus, looping it, and building your verses around this anchor. It allows you to play with the arrangement without losing the core vibe.

Sampling, on the other hand, opens a universe of sounds. Picture this: you're walking through the park, and the sound of leaves crunching beneath your feet catches your attention. Record it. That sound could become a unique percussive element in your next track. Every day, noise can find new life in your music, adding an individualized touch.

Once you start looping and sampling, dive deeper into sound manipulation. This is where creativity takes flight. Techniques like time-stretching allow you to alter the speed of sounds without changing their pitch. This can create dreamy, elongated tones perfect for intros or atmospheric backgrounds. Then there's pitch-shifting, which lets you move sounds up or down in pitch. It can give your music a fresh voice without changing the words. Playing with reverse audio effects can also lead to some mind-bending creations. Have you ever heard a song where it sounds like time is moving backward? That's reverse audio at work, creating unique, unexpected sounds that keep listeners guessing.

Technology doesn't stop at sound creation; it revolutionizes song arrangement, too. Digital Audio Workstations (DAWs) come packed with drag-and-drop features that are perfect for rear-ranging sections of your song. Want to see how your bridge would sound as an intro? Drag it and listen. This freedom to experiment means you can easily test different structures until you find what clicks best. Visualizing your song structure using digital tools helps you see the big picture, making it easier to balance repetition and variation.

The tech doesn't end there! Artificial Intelligence (AI) and machine learning are excitingly stepping into the creative process. AI-generated chord progressions can break you out of creative ruts and suggest combinations you might not have considered. It's like having a co-writer who never runs out of ideas. Some tools even analyze your musical preferences and suggest melodies that fit your style. While these tools won't replace your creativity, they can enhance it by offering fresh perspectives and ideas you might not stumble upon alone.

Let's say you wake up with a melody in your head but are unsure how to expand it. AI tools can offer chord suggestions that align perfectly with your tune, providing a solid foundation to build.

They can function as a launchpad, giving you enough momentum to leap into new musical territories.

So, now you've got a loop playing, samples layered in, and AI-generated chords guiding your way. What once felt like creative blocks became stepping stones to something greater, driven by technology's limitless potential. Your music evolves as you intertwine human intuition with digital innovation, crafting sounds that feel familiar and fresh. Technology can be an extension of your creativity, letting you explore realms of sound you never thought possible before.

Try incorporating these techniques into your songwriting routine. You'll find that technology can expand what's possible. It encourages experimentation and invites collaboration between you and the digital world. As you embrace these tools, you'll see them as companions on your creative journey rather than mere gadgets. They'll push boundaries, spark ideas, and help bring your musical dreams to life in ways you never imagined possible.

Incorporating technology into your songwriting doesn't mean replacing traditional methods but enhancing them with new dimensions of creativity and expression. As you explore loops, samples, sound manipulation, and AI tools, let them guide you toward discovering new facets of your music-making potential. Who knows? You might stumble upon the next big sound that resonates with you and listeners worldwide.

NAVIGATING THE DIGITAL MUSIC LANDSCAPE

Today, getting your music "out there" is way easier than it used to be. Thanks to digital distribution platforms, you can share your songs with the world in just a few clicks. Take Spotify and Apple Music, for example. These platforms are like modern-day radio stations but with a more individualized touch. Artists from every corner of the globe upload their tracks, and listeners can discover them with the tap of a screen. If you're ready to share your music, platforms like TuneCore can help you get your songs on these services. They function as a bridge, taking your tunes from your computer to listeners worldwide. It's like having a virtual manager who helps you reach audiences everywhere.

Now, let's talk about the power of social media. It's not just for selfies and memes; it's also a powerhouse for promoting your music. Instagram and TikTok are two key players here. Creating content highlighting your music, like short clips of you performing or behind-the-scenes looks at your creative process, can engage fans and draw new listeners in. These platforms thrive on creativity and authenticity, so let your personality shine through.

Meanwhile, Facebook is great for building a community around your music. Start a group where fans can discuss your songs, share their thoughts, and connect over shared interests. It's all about creating a space where your music can thrive, and you can engage directly with those who support you.

Monetizing your music online is another exciting frontier. You can turn your passion into something that helps you pay the bills. Platforms like Patreon allow fans to support you directly. It's like a digital tip jar where subscribers can contribute monthly in exchange for exclusive content. It's a way to build a closer relationship with your audience while funding your creative endeavors. Then there's Bandcamp, where you can sell your music and merchandise directly to fans. It's straightforward and gives you control over pricing and presentation. Offering physical goods like T-shirts or vinyl records adds a tangible element that fans love.

Today, being informed about digital trends can be as important as making great music. The digital landscape constantly shifts, so keeping up with the latest trends will ensure you're not left behind. Follow music industry news blogs to stay updated on what's happening and what's next. These sources offer insights into changes in streaming services, emerging platforms, and shifts in listener habits. Participating in online webinars and workshops can also be incredibly valuable. They provide opportunities to gain experience from industry experts and connect with other musicians facing similar challenges.

As we wrap up this chapter on navigating the digital music landscape, remember that these tools are here to amplify your creativity, not replace it. They're designed to help you reach broader audiences and deepen connections with fans who love what you do. Each platform, whether for distribution or promotion, acts as an extension of your artistry, allowing you to share your passion globally. Stay tuned for tips on stage presence, set lists, and creating unforgettable shows that will leave a lasting impact on anyone lucky enough to be in the crowd.

12

TURNING LIFE INTO LYRICS

You are chilling in your favorite spot—the park, your room, or wherever your thoughts feel free to wander. A melody plays in your head on repeat, totally your own, just waiting to be turned into something tangible. Your notebook is open, pages fluttering a little in the breeze, ready to catch every lyric, every idea. That first spark of inspiration is powerful, but turning it into a full song? That is where the real adventure begins. It mixes exciting wins and challenging moments, but every step teaches something new. In this chapter, we will talk about how to set tangible goals for your songwriting—goals that help you grow, stay motivated, and bring your music to life accurately.

SETTING PERSONAL SONGWRITING GOALS

Setting goals for your songwriting is like making a playlist for your creative journey—it helps you know where you are headed and keeps things on track. Think about what you want to accomplish soon, like writing three songs that capture your feelings this month. Or maybe you have a bigger dream, like dropping your first EP next year that shows off your one-of-a-kind sound. These goals give your creativity direction and help you stay focused and motivated.

The key is to break those big dreams into smaller, doable steps. Try setting up a weekly schedule—maybe Tuesday afternoons become your lyric-writing time, or Sunday nights are all about messing with new chord progressions. You could also set aside a few hours to work on specific skills, like developing better hooks or trying different song structures. These little goals make the big ones feel less overwhelming—and way more possible. Plus, you will know you are making progress every time you finish a session.

And here is the thing: your goals do not have to stay the same forever. Life can throw surprises your way, and your music will grow and shift with you. You discover a new genre that lights you up, or something unexpected changes your vibe. It is okay to adjust your goals. It is smart. Your plans should grow with you and reflect who you are now, not just who you were when you first made them.

Do not forget to celebrate your wins, no matter how big or small. Finishing a song? That is a big deal! You could play it for a few close friends, have a mini listening party, or blast it through your speakers and enjoy the moment. Keep a journal or digital log to track your progress—looking back and seeing how far you have come is incredible. Every step forward counts, and each one is a part of your songwriting journey.

Interactive Element: Goal-Setting Reflection

Take a quiet moment for introspection to consider what you aspire to achieve with your songwriting over the next year. Look deeply within yourself and draft short-term and long-term goals. Under each goal, outline the precise, actionable steps to guide you toward achieving it. Keep this written list where you can readily see it, whether on your desk or as a note on your smartphone. As you advance, make it a habit to check off tasks you've completed and make necessary adjustments to your goals as they evolve. This reflective exercise will guide you, maintain your focus and motivation, and transform your aspirations into tangible realities.

CONTINUOUS LEARNING AND ADAPTATION

Every songwriter knows deep down that music is more than sounds and lyrics—it is alive. It moves, grows, and tells stories. A growth mindset is one of the best tools on this creative ride. That means seeing challenges not as things that stop you, but as things that help you level up.

Keeping up with what is happening in the music world is like following your favorite show—something new is always happening. Listen to music podcasts, scroll through blogs, or watch YouTube creators discussing the latest trends, tech, and creative tips. You will pick up inspiration everywhere you can, such as going to a songwriting workshop or music event. Not only will you learn a ton, but you will also meet other people who love music just like you do. You will learn while making connections that will fuel your creativity.

Learning never really ends. There is always something new to discover, whether brushing up on music theory, exploring how to record and produce your tracks, or trying out tools you have never used. Online courses, YouTube tutorials, or even short classes can give you serious backstage access to how music works—and hearing from artists and pros who have been through it all? That kind of insight can spark ideas you never expected.

Tech is also a total game changer, as we have seen. Whether it is a new app, software, or even virtual reality, the tools you have now can help turn your songs into unforgettable experiences.

Adapting to change does not mean chasing every trend that pops up. It means figuring out what fits *you*. Use what makes sense for your style and vibe. When you mix your unique voice with tools and ideas that click, you are not just writing songs but building something that reflects who you are.

A growth mindset will help you stay open, curious, and ready to try something new. Every tough moment is a chance to grow. Every lesson you learn adds to your skills. You never know which piece will help you write your next favorite song.

As you grow as a songwriter, remember that every note you play and every lyric you write is part of your story. Stay open, keep learning, and keep creating. Your music has no limits, and neither do you.

CELEBRATING YOUR UNIQUE VOICE

Let us say you are in a room full of other songwriters, each one with their mix of ideas, experiences, and vibes. The trick to standing out as a songwriter is embracing your unique self—your beliefs, values, and experiences are the colors in your creative palette. They are what make your music unmistakably yours. When you write from your heart, sharing your moments of joy or struggle, you open a piece of who you are. Whether it is a line that captures a tough time or a melody inspired by an artist you admire, these details shape your sound and make it yours.

In a world where everyone follows trends, it can be easy to feel like you must blend in. However, real originality comes when you resist the urge to copy what has already been done. You do not have to ignore what works, but do not just repeat it. Trust your instincts—your gut will lead you to something real. Creating music that is authentic to you is what sets you apart, not just another version of something everyone's heard before. Those little personal touches, the unique twists in your style, will make you stand out.

Finding your signature style is like building your brand in music. It is about creating a sound and vibe that people can instantly recognize. Themes like resilience or freedom might keep popping up in your lyrics and will tie your songs together cohesively. Your style is not about the music, though—it is about your visuals, too. Things like album art and how you present yourself on social media are all part of the message you share with the world.

Writing from personal experience takes guts because it means being open and showing others the world through your eyes. At first, putting those emotions out there might feel scary, but it is also powerful. Writing without worrying about judgment builds connections with listeners who have been through similar stuff. Sharing the story behind your songs gives them more depth. You invite people into your world and let them understand what you created and why it means so much to you.

Now, picture yourself performing a super personal song. As the final note plays, you share the story behind it—the moment of inspiration, the vulnerability it came from. You will see the crowd nodding, feeling the connection. That is the magic of authenticity. It brings you and your listeners closer, making the music more meaningful.

Your voice is one of a kind, and it deserves to be heard. Own what makes you different and let your true self shine through every note and lyric. Trust your creative instincts, build your unique style, and confidently share your story. Your music reflects who you are and is a gift to everyone who listens.

Interactive Element: Personal Storytelling Exercise

Take a quiet moment to reflect on an experience that has profoundly impacted you—one that stirred emotions or shifted perspectives. With this memory in mind, please describe what happened, how it felt, and why it mattered. Use these reflections as inspiration for a new song. Let the memory guide your lyrics and melody, allowing your personal story to unfold through music.

INSPIRING THE NEXT GENERATION

A lively circle of young, enthusiastic musicians sits in a quaint, cozy room, each with a musical instrument in hand, their eyes gleaming with excitement and an intense eagerness to learn. They listen intently as you share your experiences—the thrilling triumphs, stumbles, and lessons learned. This is the heart of community building in music: creating an environment that thrives on creativity and is fueled by support. Offering constructive feedback to fellow songwriters is one of the most valuable gifts you can give. It is more than just pointing out weaknesses—it is about highlighting their strengths and suggesting exciting new possibilities. Your guidance can help them grow and explore new directions.

Collaboration, an essential aspect that thrives on unity, emerges as another important part of mentorship. Collaborating with younger musicians does not just help them grow—it also enriches your journey. Their fresh perspectives and innovative ideas may inspire you in ways you had not expected, reigniting creativity that might have been dormant.

Creating inclusive spaces for creative expression is central to building a community of diverse voices and talents. Organizing local songwriting meetups or open mics encourages everyone to share their art, regardless of experience level. These gatherings are vibrant hubs where unique styles and backgrounds collide, sparking endless collaboration and innovative ideas. Promoting a diverse environment ensures a rich variety of sounds and stories, allowing everyone to sit at the table and share their unique perspectives.

Music has incredible potential as a means for positive social impact. Participating in community outreach—whether through charity events or benefit concerts—can create real change. For example, performing at a local fundraiser can raise awareness and support for causes that matter deeply to you. Conducting song-writing workshops for younger audiences is another way to give back. This allows you to pass the torch, spark a passion for music in the next generation, and show them that their voices matter. By sharing your knowledge and experiences, you can inspire others to dive into their creative processes and discover their unique artistic identity.

Leading by example with integrity and passion is one of the most profound ways to inspire others. When you share your journey with its successes and challenges, you demonstrate authenticity and courage. Be transparent about the hard work and dedication required to create meaningful music. Uphold artistic integrity and stay true to your voice, even when faced with challenges or trends that might push you in different directions. Your commitment to authenticity will encourage others to pursue their artistic dreams without compromising, showing them that success is not about fame but creating real and impactful work.

As this chapter closes, reflect on the ripple effect your actions can have. By mentoring, creating inclusive spaces, using music for social good, and leading with integrity, you do more than make music—you build a community. This sense of purpose connects you to something bigger than yourself.

CONCLUSION

You have reached the end of this book, and what an experience it has been! We have explored every aspect of songwriting, uncovering how to turn your thoughts and emotions into music that speaks directly to others. When you first opened this book, unsure of what to expect, look at how far you have come. You now have the resources you need to write your songs.

Throughout these chapters, we have broken the songwriting process down into simple, manageable steps. From a blank page to a fully realized song, you have learned that songwriting is not about being a prodigy or having the latest gear. It is about discovering your voice and expressing it in a way that is authentic to you. Each step has been designed to be accessible, offering guidance with empathy and encouragement every step of the way.

The emotional connection is a central theme we have covered. You have learned how to turn your emotions into resonating lyrics, build hooks that stay with listeners, and craft melodies that linger long after the song ends. The most essential part is to make your audience feel something—joy, sadness, or empowerment. Music connects people, and your songs can be the bridge that brings them together.

We have also made music theory clear and relevant to your songwriting. You now know how to work with chords, scales, and harmonies to give your songs depth and texture. But remember, theory is just a guide—it is meant to help you express your creativity, not restrict it with rigid rules.

Creative blocks are part of every artist's path. We have looked at ways to overcome them, from prompts to shifting your environment, so you can keep your ideas flowing. Do not let blocks discourage you; view them as challenges that push you to grow and explore new paths.

Staying true to your originality and authenticity is essential. Your unique voice and experiences are what set your music apart. Embrace that! The world does not need more copies; it requires your genuine, unfiltered self.

We also discussed the importance of building a community and seeking feedback. Surrounding yourself with supportive people who offer constructive criticism helps you refine your craft and become a better songwriter. Their feedback is a gift that can guide you in new directions.

In today's digital world, technology can be an invaluable partner. Whether you are using DAWs to produce your songs or social media to share your work, technology opens endless possibilities and connects you with listeners across the globe.

Now, it is your time. Take everything you have learned and start making music. Your first song is closer than you think. Use the strategies we have discussed, and watch your ideas come to life. Remember, every great songwriter started somewhere, and you are already on the path.

As you continue your progress, keep learning and growing. Every challenge is an opportunity to evolve as a songwriter, adding new layers to your artistry. The more you create, the more you develop your style and voice.

Most importantly, always remember that your voice matters. You can impact the world through your music. Every note you play and every word you write can resonate with someone out there. So, make some noise, and let the world hear you. Your story is just beginning, and I cannot wait to see where your music takes you.

SHARE YOUR WORDS AND MAKE A DIFFERENCE!

You have done a fantastic job, and I am convinced your music will make a difference. You should be proud of your achievements and excited about what you can still accomplish. It feels good. How about we help other teens feel the same way?

YOUR OPINION MATTERS!
LEAVE A REVIEW TO HELP OTHERS JUST LIKE YOU

Thank you so much for your attention and participation. I also want to read your opinion and how you are getting on with your songwriting, so maybe you can even share your favorite lyrics you have written! Good luck and keep going! You've got this!

REFERENCES

Amuse. (2023). *Best DAWs for beginners in 2023*. https://www.amuse.io/en/categories/how-to/start-music-career/best-daws-for-beginners-in-2023

ASCAP. (n.d.). *15 essential rhyme schemes for songwriters*. https://www.ascap.com/help/career-development/15-rhyme-schemes-jordan-reynolds

Artist Weekly. (n.d.). *The rise of genre fluidity in the modern music scene*. https://artistweekly.com/the-rise-of-genre-fluidity-in-modern-music-scenes/

Audient. (n.d.). *Building a home studio (on a budget)*. https://audient.com/tutorial/building-a-home-studio-on-a-budget/

Carry a Tune. (n.d.). *The power of online music communities: A hub for artists and fans*. https://www.carryatune.in/blog/power-of-online-music-communities

Ditto Music. (n.d.). *AI for music production: 10 tools to produce like a pro*. https://dittomusic.com/en/blog/ai-for-music-production-tools-for-musicians

EDM Tips. (n.d.). *Melodies that evoke 5 emotions (how to create)*. https://edmtips.com/melodies-that-create-emotions/

Flypaper. (n.d.). *4 tips for constructive criticism in songwriting*. https://flypaper.soundfly.com/write/4-tips-for-constructive-criticism-in-songwriting/

Frederick, R. (n.d.). *Songwriting: Being authentic*. https://robinfrederick.com/being-authentic/

Frontiers in Psychology. (2017). *Emotional responses to music: Shifts in frontal brain asymmetry*. https://www.frontiersin.org/articles/10.3389/fpsyg.2017.02044/full

Full Voice Music. (n.d.). *Teaching harmony singing to beginners*. https://www.fullvoicemusic.com/teaching-harmony-singing-to-beginners/

IFPI. (2023). *Global music report 2023 – State of the industry*. https://www.ifpi.org/wp-content/uploads/2020/03/Global_Music_Report_2023_State_of-the_Industry.pdf

LAist. (n.d.). *Take a sneak peek into a legendary songwriter's creative process*. https://laist.com/news/arts-and-entertainment/take-a-sneak-peek-into-a-legendary-songwriters-creative-process

Learn by Ear. (n.d.). *Finding your voice as a songwriter – Lessons on authenticity and originality*. https://learnbyear.io/blog/songwriting-finding-voice-lessons-authenticity-originality-pros

Life Skills Advocate. (n.d.). *15 strategies for cultivating a growth mindset in teens & adults*. https://lifeskillsadvocate.com/blog/15-strategies-to-help-teens-adults-overcome-a-fixed-mindset/

Lyric Song Chords. (n.d.). *The impact of culture and society on songwriting*. https://lyricsongchords.com/blog/the-impact-of-culture-and-society-on-songwriting

MakeMusic. (n.d.). *Using S.M.A.R.T. goals to achieve musical excellence*. http://www.makemusic.com/blog/using-smart-goals-to-achieve-musical-excellence/

Masterpiece Society. (n.d.). *Help your teen overcome creative blocks*. https://masterpiecesociety.com/help-teen-overcome-creative-blocks/

Music Mecca. (2024). *Year in review: Top 10 genre-bending artists of 2024*. https://musicmecca.org/year-in-review-top-10-genre-bending-artists-of-2024/

Musicnotes. (n.d.). *The art of bridge: 12 songs with memorable bridges*. https://www.musicnotes.com/blog/the-art-of-the-bridge-12-songs-with-memorable-bridges/

Musicnotes. (n.d.). *The art of lyric writing: How to match lyrics to melody*. https://www.musicnotes.com/blog/art-lyric-writing-match-lyrics-melody/

MusicTheory.net. (n.d.). *Lessons*. https://www.musictheory.net/lessons

Musicmap. (n.d.). *The genealogy and history of popular music genres*. https://musicmap.info/

Native Instruments. (n.d.). *5 essential pop chord progressions and how to use them*. https://blog.native-instruments.com/pop-chord-progressions/

Neuroscience News. (n.d.). *Hooks and earworms: What makes pop songs so catchy?* https://neurosciencenews.com/music-earworms-hooks-22322/

Nonoki. (n.d.). *Building a thriving support network for artists*. https://nonoki.com/blog/building-a-support-network-for-artists/

PMC. (n.d.). *Songs tell a story: The arc of narrative for music*. https://pmc.ncbi.nlm.nih.gov/articles/PMC11098490/

PMC. (n.d.). *The influence of natural environments on creativity*. https://pmc.ncbi.nlm.nih.gov/articles/PMC9363772/

Revart. (n.d.). *The importance of a growth mindset for artists: Embrace challenges and foster creativity*. https://revart.co/blogs/179_The_Importance_of_a_Growth_Mindset_for_Artists_Embrace_Challenges_and_Foster_Creativity

School of Rock. (n.d.). *9 best vocal warm-ups for singers*. https://www.schoolofrock.com/resources/vocals/9-best-vocal-warm-ups-for-singers

Sonicbids. (n.d.). *4 music theory techniques to help you write a great chorus*. https://blog.sonicbids.com/4-music-theory-techniques-to-help-you-write-a-great-chorus

Soundwell Music Therapy. (n.d.). *Music-based mindfulness exercises: 4 ways to be, hear, now*. https://soundwellmusictherapy.com/music-as-mindfulness-exercises/

Sounds Familiar. (n.d.). *The anatomy of a hit song: What makes a hit, a hit?* https://www.soundsfamiliar.co/post/the-anatomy-of-a-hit-song-what-makes-a-hit-a-hit

Spencer Education. (n.d.). *Ten strategies to crush self-doubt in creative work*. https://spencereducation.com/10-strategies-creative-doubt/

Splice. (n.d.). *20 songwriting apps and books that will level up your music*. https://splice.com/blog/songwriting-apps-and-books/

StudySmarter. (n.d.). *Harmony techniques: Analysis & exercises*. https://www.studysmarter.co.uk/explanations/music/music-composition/harmony-techniques/

StudySmarter. (n.d.). *Musical storytelling: Technique & examples*. https://www.studysmarter.co.uk/explanations/music/music-composition/musical-storytelling/

The Gear Page. (n.d.). *Hit songs with "unusual" arrangements*. https://www.thegearpage.net/board/index.php?threads/hit-songs-with-unusual-arrangements.2532089/

The Schwartz Scene. (2021, July 1). *By the light of metaphor: A Stephen Schwartz interview*. https://www.theschwartzscene.com/2021/07/01/by-the-light-of-metaphor-a-stephen-schwartz-interview/

UJAM. (2025). *The top 10 trends shaping the music industry in 2025*. https://www.ujam.com/blog/the-top-10-trends-shaping-the-music-industry-in-2025/

Unizin. (n.d.). *Music and emotional intelligence*. https://ufl.pb.unizin.org/mandhdevelopment/chapter/music-and-emotional-intelligence/

Vironika. (n.d.). *Famous people who refused to be destroyed by criticism*. https://www.vironika.org/criticism/

Vocal Media. (n.d.). *The creative influence of lyrics on songwriting*. https://vocal.media/fyi/the-creative-influence-of-lyrics-on-songwriting

wikiHow. (n.d.). *How to write songs as a teenager: 10 steps (with pictures)*. https://www.wikihow.com/Write-Songs-As-a-Teenager

Writing Institute. (n.d.). *Creating a sustainable writing routine*. https://www.writinginstitute.pitt.edu/writingroutine

Yamaha Music. (n.d.). *Making the perfect creative space*. https://hub.yamaha.com/brand/creativity/making-the-perfect-creative-space/

Yousician. (n.d.). *Characteristics of music genres – Learn to play different styles*. https://yousician.com/blog/music-genres

www.ingramcontent.com/pod-product-compliance
Lightning Source LLC
Chambersburg PA
CBHW031430120626
46545CB00006B/2333